Porcelain Painting

Porcelain Painting

with Uwe Geissler

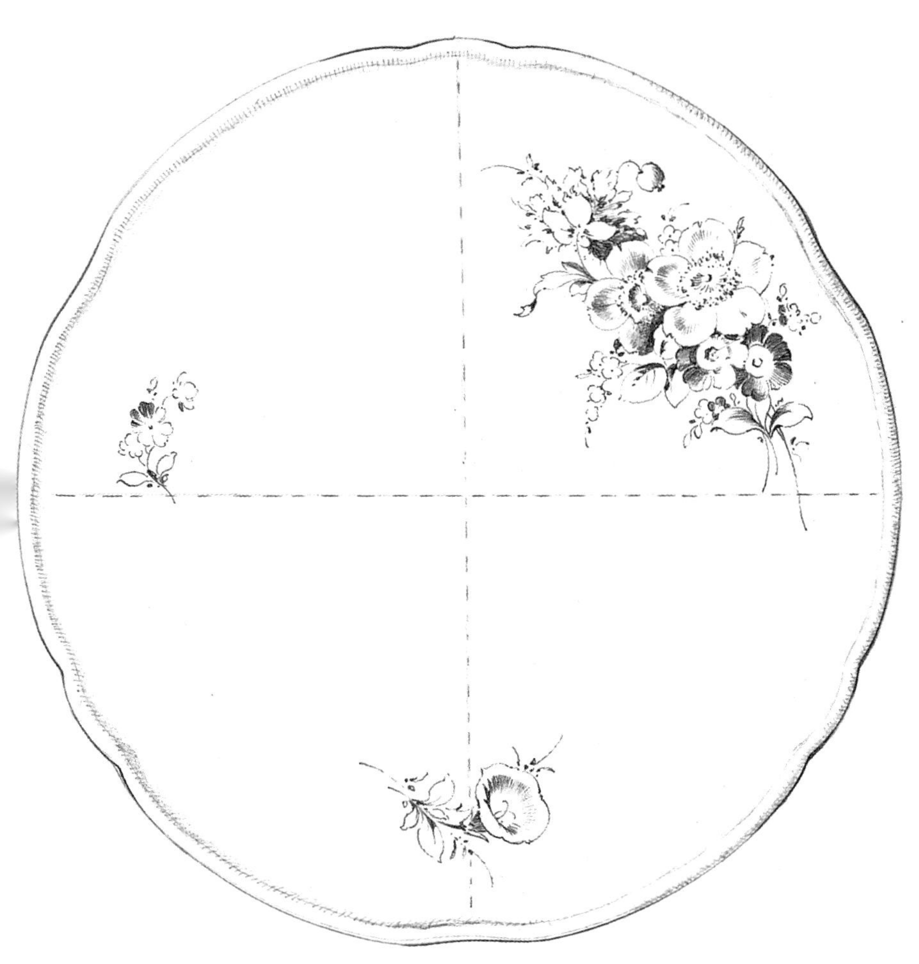

4880 Lower Valley Road • Atglen, PA 19310

Translated by Dr. Edward Force,
Central Connecticut State University
Cover Design by Baur + Belli, Munich, using
a drawing by the author.

Original German language third edition
published 1992 by Verlag Georg D.W.
Callwey, München.

ISBN: 978-0-88740-899-1

Printed in China

Library of Congress Cataloging-in-Publication Data

Geissler, Uwe.
[Porzellan bemalen. English]
Porcelain painting with Uwe Geissler.
p. cm.
Includes bibliographical references.
ISBN 0-88740-899-0 (paper)
1. China painting--Technique. I. Title.
NK4605.G4213 1995
738.1'5--dc20 95-31098
CIP

Published by Schiffer Publishing, Ltd.
4880 Lower Valley Road
Atglen, PA 19310
Please write for a free catalog.
This book may be purchased from the publisher.
Try your bookstore first.

We are interested in hearing from authors with book ideas on related subjects.

THE AUTHOR

worked for eleven years at the State Porcelain Factory in Meissen, and has been a decor designer and teacher of painting courses in Cologne since 1984. International exhibitions. Publications: "Porzellanmalerei—Rosen," "Porzellan bemalen heute," "Porzellan bemalen auf Meissner Art."

Uwe Geissler
Haupt Strasse 76
51503 Rösrath
Germany

Hearty thanks for their help and support in the completion of this book to
The W. Goebel firm
Hanns Welling
Klaus
Manu
Danni, and
Maestro Sigi Wendler

CONTENTS

FOREWORD 7

MATERIALS 8
Whiteware 8
Painting Tools 10
—Brushes 10
—Oils 10
—Paints 11
—Palettes, Spatulas, Palette Knives 12
—Crayons and Brush Handles 13

THE WORKBENCH 14

FIRING PAINTED PORCELAIN 16

BEFORE PAINTING 18
Loosening-up Practices 18
Preparing the Piece 18
Composing the Decor 18
Preparing the Paint 20

FLOWER PAINTING 22
Nature Studies 22
Rose Painting 26
Manneristic Painting 29
Asters 29
Hedgeroses 30
Bouquet and Greenery Painting 39
Scattered Flowers 45
Edges and Tendrils 50

BACKGROUND FORMATION 52
Quiet Backgrounds for Still-Lifes and Portraits 52
Blanking Medallion Surfaces 52
Other Backgrounds 53

NATURALISTIC PAINTING 56
Fruits 57
Insects 59
Birds 60
Animals 63
Landscape Painting 64
Individual Buildings 65
Christmas Plates 69
Children's Motifs 70
Copperplate Painting 74

FANTASY DESIGNS 76
Decorative Motifs 81
Ornaments 81
Stylized Flowers 87
Edge Decorations 88

INDIAN AND FAR EASTERN PAINTING 92
Equipment 93
The Stencil 97
Drawing with the Pen 97
Stylized Flowers and Birds 98
—Pheasant with Flowers 99
—Stylized Flowers 99
Stylized Animals, Dragons, and Mythical Creatures 100

GOLD DECORATION 104
Gloss Gold 104
Polished Gold 104
Powdered Gold 104
Brushes 104
Border Discs 106
—Drawing Lines with the Border Disc 106
—Painting the Border 106
Framing Medallions and Backgrounds 106
Gold Borders 106
Decorating Handles, Spouts, and Knobs 108
Gilding Pierced Porcelain 109

PLATINUM DECORATION 110

MONOGRAMS 110

SIGNETS 114

FINISHED PORCELAIN PAINTING 116

GLOSSARY 126

BIBLIOGRAPHY 127

PHOTO CREDITS 127

FOREWORD

Much has already been written and spoken about porcelain painting, and attempts have often been made to acquaint the layman with this subject, especially in recent years since porcelain painting is finding its way into more and more households. Unfortunately, many of these guidebooks and portrayals content themselves with results that conclude with moderate "rural painting." In this book, I would like to attempt to illustrate steps for both the beginner and the advanced painter to follow to completion.

Everyone must decide for themselves how far their ability and talent will take them. The prerequisites—as in so many other handicraft activities—are, naturally, inspiration and a equal amount of energy. Without them, one would probably never attain success in any artistic endeavor. Here too, one may at times reach a point at which one says: "You'll never make it!" But tenacity and, above all interest, often awakens slumbering talents. In fact, at the beginning it is not important to be artistically active at once. Instead, the learning of techniques and practice with color and oil create a solid basic knowledge at the start.

When the technique has been mastered and you are able to reproduce several good "models" properly, then it is time for your own designs and studies. Surely one can put ideas on paper at any time, but to transfer them to the porcelain, one must first have mastered the painting technique, and this is not simple. It is comparable to watercolor painting, although more "corrections" can be made on porcelain. The transparency that shines through and the effect of the white background make the two techniques very similar.

Porcelain painting is also fascinating for those who have previously worked only with other techniques. Glass painters in particular will encounter many familiar and similar concepts.

I would like to try to cover the whole range of subjects and deal with all the refinements, even if they may appear to be familiar to one or another reader already.

I would like to deliberately leave out subjects concerning the production and special features, as well as the history of "white gold." There is enough specialized literature that can provide

sive amount of energy. Truly high-quality porce-

information about these topics, and interested parties can obtain information about the composition and chemical state of porcelain at any time, for porcelain has long since lost its mysterious character. Its basic composition is known all over the world today.

What with the great variety of possible designs, I would like to concentrate particularly on the classic types but also take up the subject of modern designs. For us, the focal point will be flower painting, in both manneristic and naturalistic style. In addition, we will discuss Far Eastern motifs, and landscapes and surface decor will also be discussed.

I would also like to avoid getting into the exact definitions and chemical details of ceramic paints, since a great variety of different palettes are available in the trade today, and one gets good information when purchasing them. Often enough, you can even get free samples from the manufacturers and judge their quality by using them yourself, mixing them with each other, and firing them experimentally. By keeping to the specified firing temperature and following certain rules of paint mixing, you can expect that not much could really go wrong.

In my ten years of experience at the Meissen factory and my present activity as a decor developer and instructor, I believe I have gained a not inconsiderable amount of experience, and I would be happy if I could assist the reader in attaining his goal of learning the techniques of high-quality porcelain painting in a short time. The learner, however, must contribute the decilain painting is the result of a very sensitive technique, a thing that requires feeling and devotion. If these are present and the necessary amount of talent is awakened, one can achieve beauty in the successful decoration of that noble substance, porcelain. And not least, the results should offer something unique to the beholders, something in which they, along with the artist, can take great pleasure.

Uwe Geissler

MATERIALS

White Gold

All white porcelains, such as are available in many shapes, sizes and qualities in department stores, specialty shops and antique shops, are suitable for painting. Many manufacturers of porcelain also sell directly to private customers. Catalogues and brochures offer advance information about prices and delivery dates. Here is a list of the most frequently used dishes and their usual sizes:

Mocha Set	
Mocha coffeepot	0.6 liter (l)
Mocha cup (with saucer)	0.10 l
Cake plate	15 cm diameter
Milk pitcher	0.15 l
Sugar bowl	0.15 l

Tea Set	
Teapot	0.4 l; 1.3 l
Teacup (with saucer)	0.2 l
Cake plate	16 cm; 19 cm
Milk pitcher	0.25 l
Sugar bowl	0.25 l

Coffee Set	
Coffeepot	0.9-1.3 l
Coffee cup (with saucer)	0.2 l
Cake plate	19 cm
Milk pitcher	0.25 l
Sugar bowl	0.25 l
Pastry platter	28 cm
Large cake plate	35-50 cm
Egg cup	ca. 4 cm
Warmer	variable

Dinner Set	
Plate, flat	19, 26, 28 cm
Plate	32 cm
Deep-dish plate	0.25 l
Soup cup (with saucer)	0.25 l
Tureen (soup, meat or fish dishes)	1.5 l
Gravy boat	0.4 l
Salad bowl	17, 20, 26, 28 cm
Oval platters	32, 36 cm
Salt and pepper shakers	no standard size
Fruit bowl	0.25 l

1 White porcelain for painting is available in great variety, not only in specialty shops, but also in household-goods and department stores. This picture shows an assortment manufactured by W. Goebel of Oeslau.

Individual pieces
Candleholder, jewelry boxes, candy dishes

One can see that a wealth of porcelain dishes is available for decoration. It is also especially charming to look for individual pieces at antique shops or flea markets and to make them even more valuable with high-quality painting. Of course, such a piece may be decorated already; it might, for example, have a gold rim. Renewed firing almost never damages the old paint.

Before the amateur painter ventures to paint costly porcelain from world-famous factories, he should practice on lower-priced goods. Under no circumstances should he forget to place his own symbol or signature on the underside of the porcelain piece. This can be a signature, a coat of arms, or symbol. In addition, the date and a reference to hand-painting should be added. The English term "handpainted" has made itself at home in Germany. For this, one usually uses red, cobalt blue, or gold. The main symbol is, as a rule, located in the center of the bottom. Smaller additions such as the date, pattern name, or dedication can also be placed on the rim of the bottom.

2 Dishes with relief patterns are often charming subjects for painting. Fine gold painting may also be added to the raised areas.

Painting Tools

Brushes

For actual painting, one does not need as much equipment as the layman often believes. The most important things are, of course, the brushes. Here the quill brushes with natural hair have proved themselves. Among all the types of hair that are used, from marten to cattle to various types of squirrels, the type of squirrel called "Feh" in German has turned out to be most suitable, and not just in Meissen.

Since these quill brushes have been machine-made, it frequently happens that individual hairs are attached backwards, meaning with the cut-off surface forward and the natural end bound. These "black sheep" make themselves known during painting in a particularly disturbing way when they project from the side of the brush and paint unwanted lines. For that reason it is advisable to cut these hairs out before painting. To be sure, this takes some time and patience, but it pays off later in the form of a flowing stroke. One dips the brush in some thick oil (see below, under *Oils*) and carefully presses it on a plate or a clean tile until it spreads out. When one looks closely, one can clearly see the thicker hairs without points, and can cut them out with the palette knife, which will be described in detail below. The result is an ideal brush with an excellent point. For the different types of painting, we naturally need different types or sizes of brushes. The size of the brush should vary along with the size of the flower or other motif to be painted. A typical assortment of some six sizes, though, will be completely sufficient. With appropriate use and care, many brushes will give good service for half a year, even when used every day! For that reason, one should never twist the brushes or bend them sideways. Every brush will repay you for careful use by lasting a long time. This is surely important for reasons of cost too, since the prices of natural-hair brushes have been continually rising in recent years. If a brush has not been used in a long time, then it is a good idea to wash it out in turpentine and put it in a brush box dampened with some oil of cloves. A flat sheet-metal box, in which a piece of cardboard saturated with oil of cloves is placed, is useful. Kept this way, the brush is immediately ready for use again, even after months. The most useful types of brushes are shown on the next page.

Hair brushes must be fitted onto brush handles. It is a point of honor among all good porcelain painters to prepare these handles personally. The wood of the priest's-hat bush is most suitable, but other types of soft wood are also usable. A sharp knife can be used for raw cutting, and a piece of sandpaper smooths the handle. At least three handle thicknesses are advisable, since the diameters of the brushes also vary (Ill. 6, 7).

Oils

Much could be said about the painting medium, defined in short, oil. The variety of the balsams, tinctures, and other media used often confuses even the specialist. For painting porcelain, though, the types that have been used for several hundred years suffice. The figures, scenery and various surface decorations naturally need several additional oils, since their technique is different. But the tried and true turpentine oil, in various consistencies, is enough for us. Turpentine has the characteristic, praiseworthy for porcelain painting, of "creeping away" over the rim of the container it is kept in, which can be explained by the high surface tension of this oil. In this process, the oil thickens gradually, and the irreplaceable thick oil comes into being. So one need only put turpentine in a relatively small container, and place that in turn on something like a saucer, and the required painting oil or thick oil will result all by itself. But if this process takes too long, one can apply a little heat to the turpentine, and it will "creep" somewhat faster. It is always advisable to let some turpentine age by itself in a quiet place, so as to have clean thick oil on hand at any time. Today many factories use oil that they obtain already thickened, but why should one not take the trouble of upholding one of the remaining painting traditions? (Ill. 16)

Now you need some spirits or other kind of thinner in which to wash out the brushes before changing colors. Here it must be mentioned that such natural thinners harm the brushes very much, in that they remove the natural fats from them and thus make them stiff and liable to break.

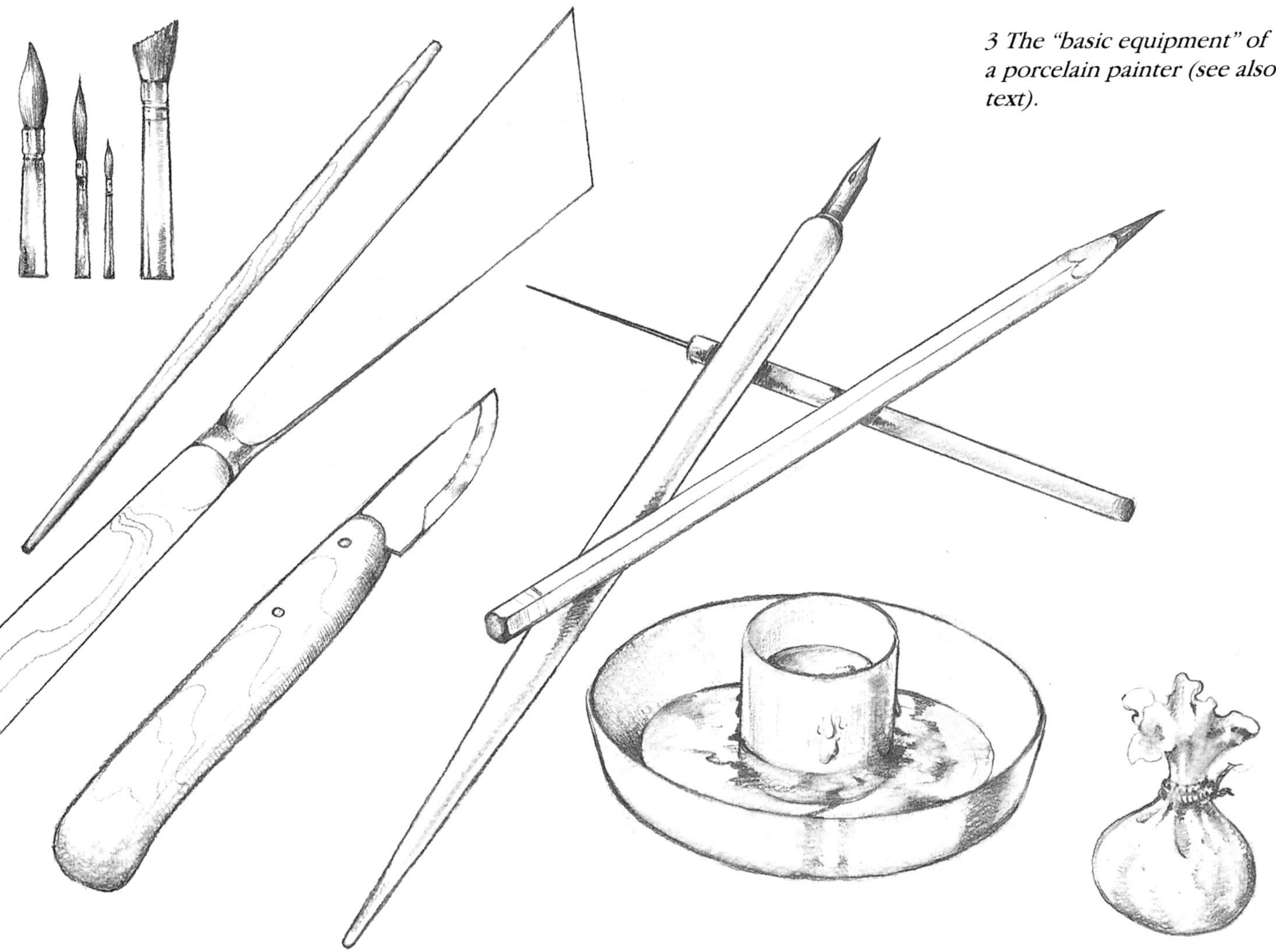

3 The "basic equipment" of a porcelain painter (see also text).

For that reason, it is also better to use turpentine for this purpose. If you have a different brush available for each color, then this problem is solved. But you cannot get along completely without spirits or thinner, since you must rub the white pieces before beginning to paint them to remove all grease and dirt. Spirits are also better than turpentine for a thorough cleaning of the spatula and the palette knife.

Now about oil of cloves, which is used above all else to keep the paint looking fresh over long periods. What with its natural characteristics, it does not dry out as quickly as other oils, and thus is keeps the paints usable for a long time, particularly in the hole palette. For painting itself, though, it is only useful in a very limited way, since it "pushes" the paint very much and thus makes definite lines difficult. It is better suited to stippling smooth surfaces or for mixing and working with turpentine. Later there will be more to say about it when we discuss using the spatula.

Paints

For the most part, these are metal oxide pigments in powdered form, which are sold in small containers, bags, glasses or tubes. I personally recommend that you buy these paints only in powdered form and mix them yourself, so as to get the feel of the paint-and-oil mix, which can and must be different for various techniques. When you buy, also find out about the lead and other poison content, in case the painted objects are used for eating. There are, in fact, very bright-colored paints of high luminosity that are not suitable for eating utensils because of their lead content. Wall platters, figures, vases, and the like can be painted with them without concern. The danger of lead does not consist of simply touching the objects, but of the reaction of, for example, vinegar, spicy sauces, fish, etc. combined with the paint.

Of all the many paint shades and tones that are on the market, only a certain basic palette,

4 The use of the palette knife: out of a completely painted rose, light effects are cut with the knife, giving the flower plasticity and a high degree of perspective. It is important to work out the transitions in the places where the contrast between bright and dark is especially great (such as in the center, on the overlappings on the shadowed side, and where one flower touches others in a bouquet). Small painting errors can also be removed easily after drying.

from which, with growing experience, many additional shades can be mixed, is necessary. Experience blends with the ground rules of mixing and can be tested in a few trial firings, on which more will be said in *Preparing the Paint.*

Palettes, Spatulas, Palette Knives

Mixing paint and preserving it for several work days can also be done in different ways. The most common is by using a simple glass palette measuring about 15 by 10 centimeters. There is also the possibility of using a separate palette for each color used and keeping them in a so-called "palette slider"—which is a long, very shallow drawer in the worktable. Since this would be too laborious for the layman, I would suggest a homemade palette box, in which there is a separate space for each palette, the palettes being only about 5 mm thick. It is very simple to make out of cardboard or thin wood, and allows the housing of several individual palettes with the paints being used.

This type of palette, though, allows the use of only one, to at most three, different colors at the same time, since the individual palettes take up a good deal of space on the worktable. In addition, it is necessary to prepare every color fresh every day. This is an advantage for painters who need only one and the same color for a long period. This will be the case primarily for painters who work at porcelain factories. But for work processes in which several colors are applied at the same time, these glass palettes are not ideal. For naturalistic flower and fruit painting, or painting of just a few pieces in one day, the so-called hole palettes are more suitable. These consist of approximately 12 x 20 cm surfaces made with depressions to hold the paint. They are made, among other materials, of plastic or ceramics. Thus one can keep about twenty colors ready to use in a relatively small space, and one need only stir them on the next work day. Naturally it is important to have the right proportion of oil and pigment, for otherwise the paint can dry out or thicken in the hole palette.

The pigment color is mixed with the oil by a spatula, which can be bought in a wide variety of types and sizes. Without a doubt, the best for our purposes is a soft but sharp steel spatula with a diagonal blade and wooden handle. Illustration 3 shows the ideal shape for our purposes.

Glass "runners" or mortars are often used as well, but this technique is better suited to mixing a large quantity of a relatively thin paint, suitable for use, for example, with a spray gun. The mixture of pigment and oil is mixed in the heavy glass mortar until a creamy and smoothly flowing condition is attained, which guarantees good further use.

The horn spatula is also seen often, but to me it seems generally unsuitable, though useful for the application of gold decoration, since the iron material of the metal spatula can rub off and cause trouble.

The palette knife (a pin is also widely used) should be a small, short knife with a short, curved blade on one side. A good point is important, as is a sharp blade without notches. The palette knife is very important to create effective points of light in painting by removing some of the already applied paint in certain places, so as to emphasize leaf surfaces or contours. The point of a pin, on the other hand, can only be used to make very thin lines in an area of paint. If one tries to work on more of the surface, one all too often scratches it. An example is shown in Illustration 4.

Crayons and Pen Handles

To draw the decorative motif on the porcelain, a readily available crayon for smooth surfaces such as glass, plastic, and porcelain is suitable. It is important that it should not make too dark and heavy a mark, since this would later result in unwanted dark color shades when coming into contact with the paint. These do burn out later, but they can disturb the painting process; a crayon that makes a soft gray mark is thus more suitable.

Pens and pen handles are no great problem. There is a wide variety of steel pens on the market, of which one with a good point is sufficient. Careful treatment of the point with fine sandpaper is recommended to remove the rough edges resulting from manufacture.

practical
ɿement of the
ment makes
cal work
ɔle.

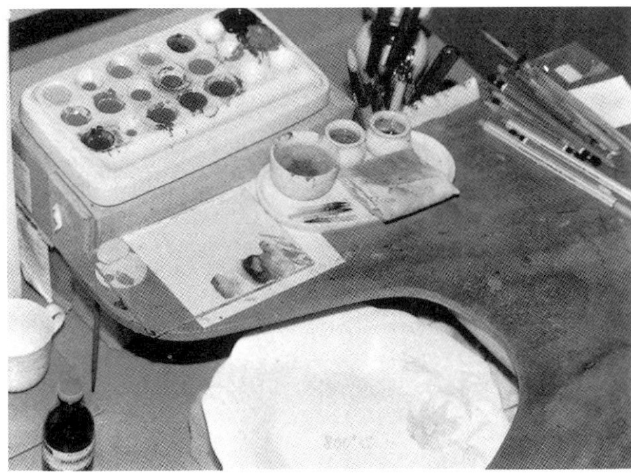

5△

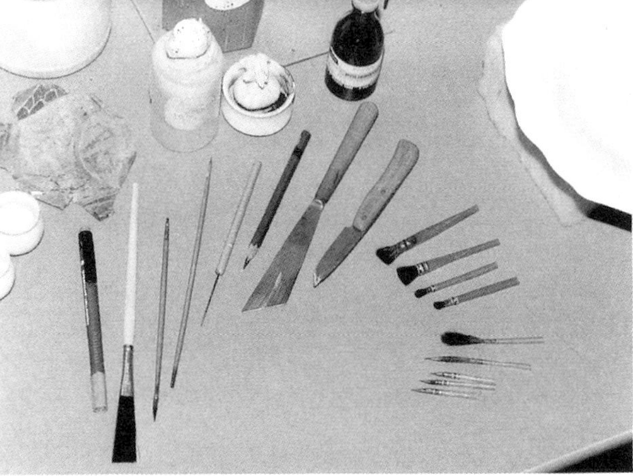

6△

7▽

e various
ment for
ain painting
e see:
palette with
d pigment; 2
palette for
painting
ous brushes
ush handles
ious metal
nts (gold and
im); 5
ic pigments
vdered form
ia for
ng (oils,
rs); 7 Stencil
Oil thickener
te knife,
, spatula
ld-polishing
(glass fibers)
ush bench on
to put
s down; 12
porcelain

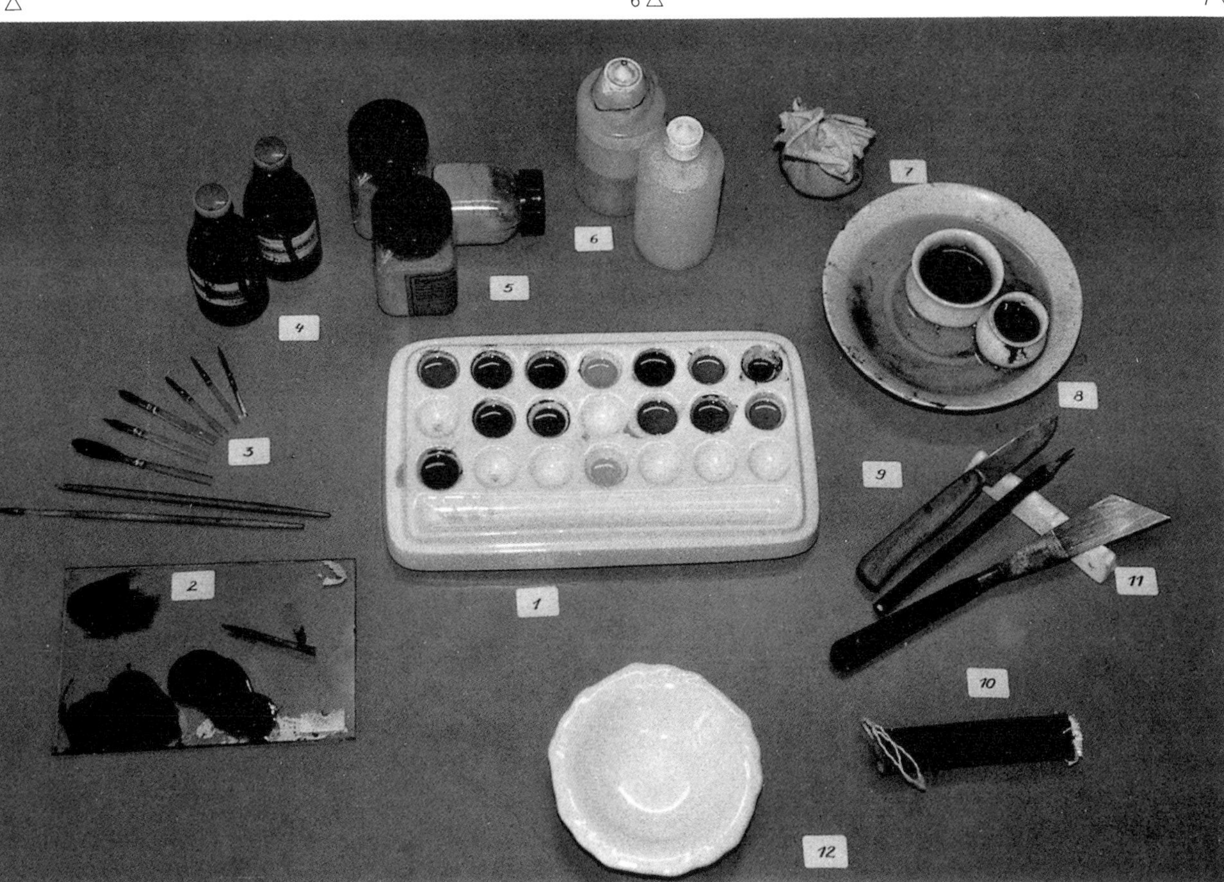

THE WORKBENCH

For good porcelain painting, the work area is just as important as paint and brushes. In the many different porcelain factories and businesses, there is a great variety of variations. Even the divergent techniques needed to paint various objects demands this. For painting dishes, the so-called "Malpult" armrest is recommended. It consists simply of a raised surface for the arm that holds the paintbrush, under which the object to be painted is held (Ill. 9). This means that the left arm, which holds the object, lies on the tabletop and makes for a steady seat for the dish, while the right arm, which does the painting, rests somewhat higher on the armrest. In the U-shaped cutout of the armrest one can paint very precisely in a steady position. The exact position is shown in Illustration 10.

Since objects of different sizes will be painted, it is ideal if the height of the armrest can be adjusted. In some factories the armrest is therefore mounted on a metal frame and held by a rod on its right side to the tubular frame of the table, where it is held in place by two wing bolts. After loosening these bolts, one can raise or lower it to the desired height, 10 centimeters for plates or 30 cm for bowls. For the hobby painter, the fixed armrest, some 12 to 15 cm high, will have to do (Ill. 8).

It can be created very simply and inexpensively. The surface with the U-shaped cutout forms the top. Now the three sides just need to be attached, so the entire piece will stand level on the table. The size and shape can be seen in Illustration 8.

Around the work space, palette, brushes, oil, and the rest should be arranged so that using them is not unnecessarily difficult. For example, there is an old rule among porcelain painters to keep the path from brush to oil and brush to paint to palette as short as possible. This rule-of-thumb arose from the introduction of payment by piecework in many shops and the resulting efforts to save time while "fetching color" with the brush. One could not save time while painting a piece; that would have cost in terms of quality. For the hobby painter, of course, this rule is unimportant. If one uses individual glass palettes, each with only one color, then the ideal sequence of arrangement around the armrest from left to right is: glass palette—oil—rest for brushes, crayon, spatula, etc. In this arrangement, one has the palette right in front of oneself and thus always has an overview of color strength and greasiness. One more tip: Always put a piece of white paper under the glass palette. Thus you can always see in what intensity the paint is going onto the object, where the white background will have its effect.

When you use the hole palette, you should set it on a suitable base above the armrest, with the glass palette in front of it on the armrest panel for mixing, and the oil and brush rest should be to the right of it. This arrangement has proved practical for porcelain painters for decades. When painting figures or underglaze, the handling of the piece and the sitting position of the painter are different.

Now you need only a few lint- and dust-free paint rags for cleaning the spatula, palette, and brushes.

Before everything is ready for painting, a few words about some healthy aspects of porcelain painting. Take care to sit straight up whenever possible. An adjustable-height chair will solve this problem, along with an adjustable armrest. Also, one should never have one's eyes too close to the object. Someone who stares at glaring white plates eight hours a day will soon notice how much of a strain this is on the eyes.

One should keep a distance of at least 20 centimeters. The blinding effect of the work light can be decreased easily by putting transparent paper in front of the source of light. Naturally, it is best when one has enough natural light to need no artificial light. But there too, bright sunlight should be avoided.

There are people who are allergic to etherlike oils and solvents. Sometimes it helps them to wear thin cloth gloves, or to avoid the direct contact of paint with their skin. Should difficulties still occur, it is best to see one's doctor. Thorough washing of one's hands after contact with oil or lead-base paint, of course, should be done in any case.

8 The armrest is easy to make and ideal for the beginner.

9 The adjustable panel is attached to the table frame by two wing nuts.

10 Along with a perfectly laid out worktable, one needs not only an armrest and the painting tools, but also a lamp to work by, and if possible a back wall, not only for placing the oils, brush handles, etc., but also for attaching patterns, sketches or photos.

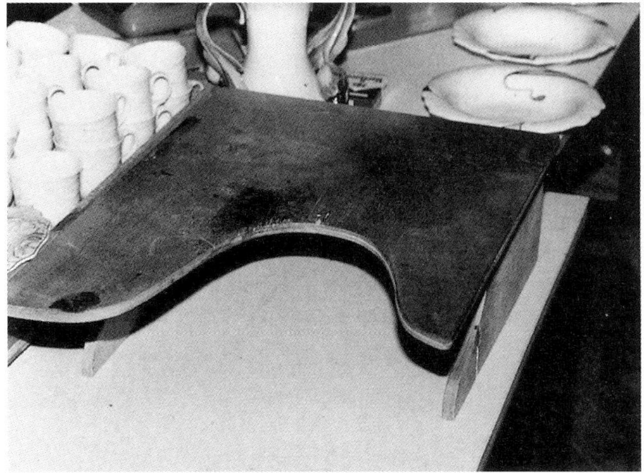

8 △

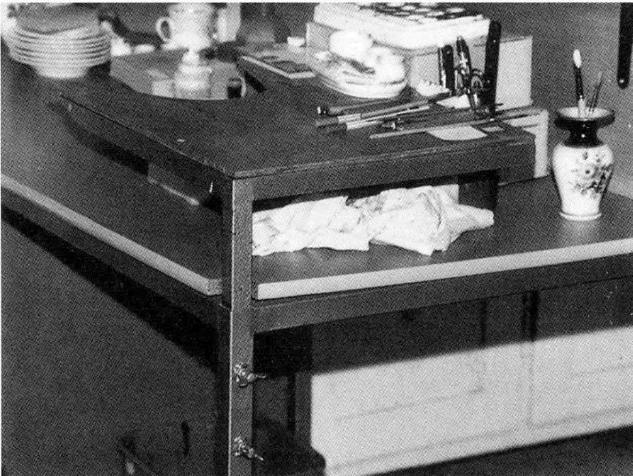

9 △

10 ▽

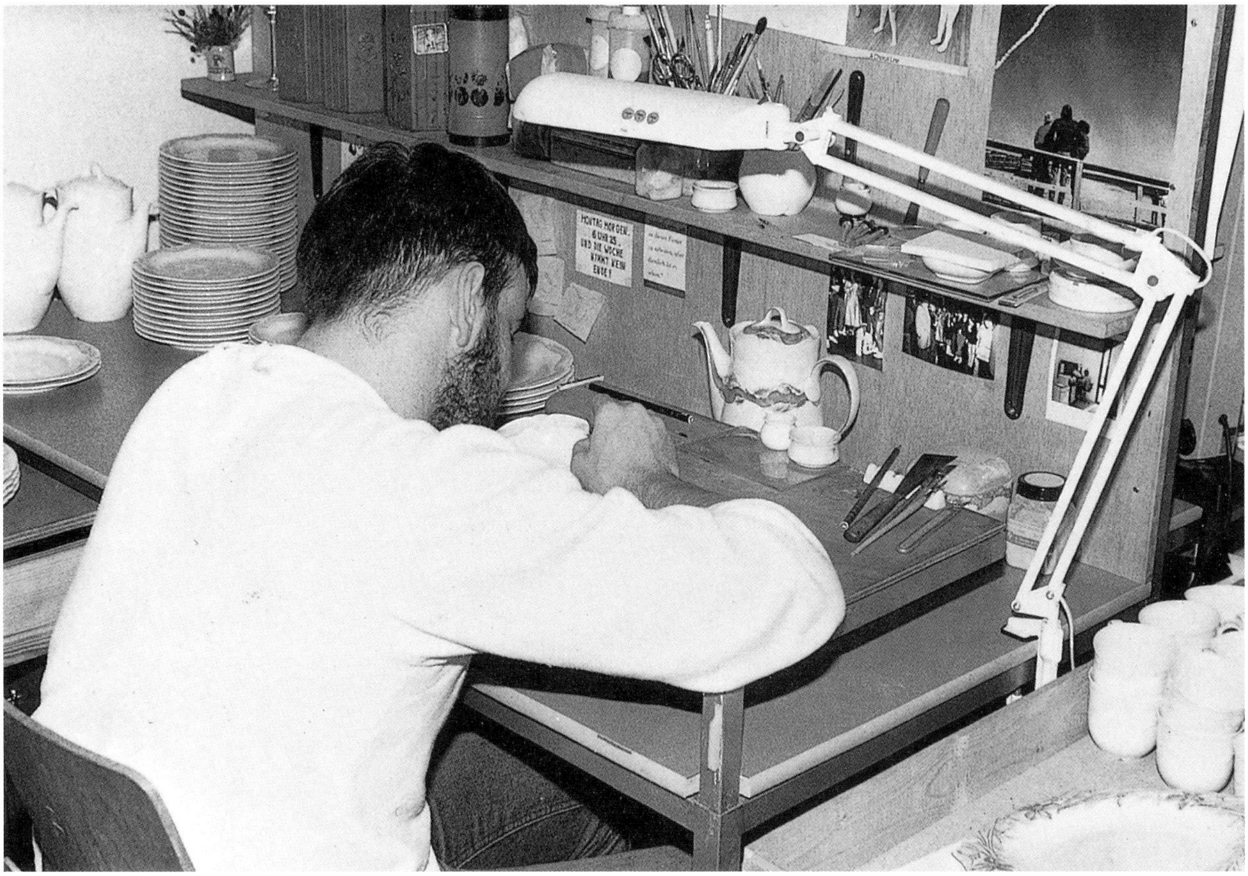

FIRING THE PAINTED PORCELAIN

Once we have the decoration, gilding (see *Gilding Pierced Porcelain*), and the final check behind us, it is time to turn to the firing of the objects. Here, each palette of colors requires its own temperature. But since the metal-oxide paints are best melted at about 800° C, this calls for no particularly great effort. The most important ground rules can be summed up here:

—It is no great problem to create a clean atmosphere in the kiln, by guaranteeing a supply of clean air coming into the assay furnace. It often occurs that in one kiln there will be several ceramically different articles being fired. This has the disadvantage that a polluted atmosphere can make faults appear on the porcelain. For that reason, coarse ceramics must be fired separately from painted porcelain.

—Proceed according to the assay furnace at your disposal. There are furnaces that will melt according to the so-called firing curve. This has the advantage that you can increase the heat slowly, without the risk of heating the piece too quickly. When the desired temperature is reached, it will be maintained for some time at the required level to guarantee an optimal firing through of the colors.

—Many sets of paints offered in the trade differ in their firing temperatures and should therefore be mixed with each other only to avoid the reactions of different paints from different manufacturers. Always use only one brand, and seek out the one that is best suited to your needs. This certainly requires several test firings, in order to see which paints will give you the best results. One simply has to understand that some manufacturers offer paints for sale that can be mixed only after a great deal of experience with the routine, so do not resign yourself to failure if the first firings are not immediately successful.

—Pay attention as well to the different types of porcelain that you encounter when you buy whiteware. The so-called bone porcelain (Fine Bone China), for example, cannot stand 800° C. On account of the relatively thin glazing, the patterns can easily be blurred at temperatures over 760° and look watery. Thus the composition of the piece has much influence on the success of the painting. But that does not mean that bone china could not stand any higher temperatures. It is just a matter of the light glazing, which becomes very liquid over 800° C and thus will scarcely preserve sharp contours.

—The smokestack, which is reached through the exhaust port in the upper surface of the furnace, must be checked out. By opening the viewing hole in the furnace door from time to time, you can free some of the exhaust of the resulting paint and oil smoke. This is especially important after the conclusion of the firing process, in order to speed up the cooling of the furnace. One must, of course, exercise caution in any premature opening of the furnace door, as it can lead quickly to cracks and breaks in the porcelain. One should absolutely not open the kiln until the temperature sinks to 300° C, since the work accomplished to that point would otherwise be endangered.

—Now a word about setting the painted pieces. One can build up several levels out of firebrick, on and in which as many pieces as possible can be set. After all, we want to utilize the available firing space optimally. But one must bear in mind that different temperatures will prevail at different places in the furnace. Place objects with particularly hard colors (purple, red, violet) toward the outside of the furnace, since the spirals of heat will have their best effect there, and those with many flowing parts (Indian painting) to the inside or in front by the door.

When you set the pieces in place, make sure that no fine splinters or fragments of the impervious plates will fall on the objects, for otherwise unwanted little pieces could be melted in and blend firmly with the glaze. Bubbles and unsightly high spots would result.

To sum up the firing process in the electric assay furnace:

a. Fill the pre-warmed assay furnace with the objects to be burned, and close the door with the viewing hole open.

b. Turn on the kiln; at about 150° C, the paints begin to vaporize; continue to keep the viewing hole open.

c. Beyond 400-450° C, the resinous components of the paints are broken down, so increase the heat.

d. Close the viewing hole and increase the temperature to the desired maximum, check the temperature on the pyrometer, turn off the heat, slowly let the furnace cool, and open the viewing hole.

e. Do not open the door at temperatures over 300° C, so as to guarantee slow cooling.

If you do not own your own kiln, entrust your painted objects to an experienced ceramic worker in your area. He will give you tips and advice, and you will learn from the results how to handle the porcelain objects correctly at the end of the firing.

11 A small assay furnace for, at most, five or six objects. It has its place in any cellar and is especially economical when used at night.

12-13 Loading a large assay furnace with painted objects on shelves. The heating coils are easy to see inside and on the door.

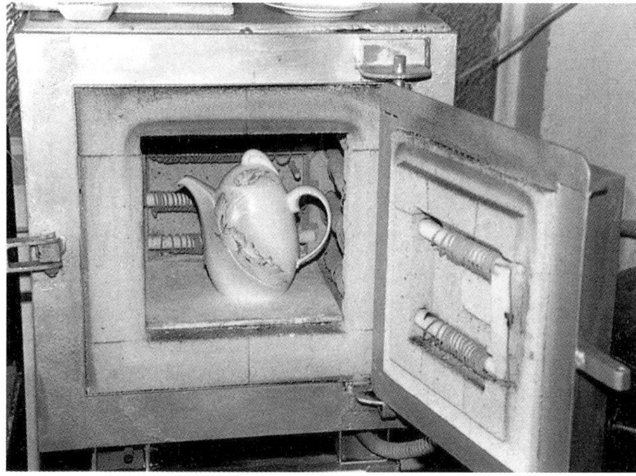

11 △

12 △

13 ▽

BEFORE FIRING

Loosening-up Processes

For any kind of painting it is a good idea to loosen up and "soften" the hand that holds the brush before one begins to paint. Making pencil sketches of any kind on paper is ideal for this purpose. On a sheet of paper begin by making large-scale curves, arcs, and ornaments, without breaking the movement of the pencil, that is, with one thing leading into another without lifting the pencil (Ill. 14-15). Make these flowing lines for about ten minutes, while at the same time taking care to divide up the surface well. Here one can already begin to practice laying out a relatively large area harmoniously. At the beginning, this step may seem somewhat boring, but it very definitely has its rewards. The hand becomes active and the brush can be controlled much better.

Preparing the Porcelain

Before one can begin to paint on the porcelain, the white surface must be thoroughly cleaned of dust and grease and then dried. Any bit of dirt can cause undesirable results during firing and spoil the painting. It is best to rub the piece with spirits and a dust-free cloth. Cleaning fluid is also suitable. Now we can examine the piece for any flaws in the structure or glazing, so that if there are any, we can try to conceal them when we paint. We may find cracks, or flecks of oxides resulting from the porcelain mass being milled with iron tools. In most cases, such flaws can be covered with a small flower figure or the like. Once we have the cleaned piece before us, we can begin to draw on it.

The Decor Pattern

To lay out the design, it is most important that the piece be evenly decorated, not with all the painting in one place, but with it distributed harmoniously. One can also—as was common in the Baroque era—overload a piece and make it very impressive, but this is left to the taste of the painter or the customer.

For the so-called flat pieces (plates, saucers, wall platters, etc.), there is always the possibility of arranging the decoration exactly in the center, or around the rim, the "flag." As for variations in the middle, one cannot do much wrong, as a central motif dominates, and it may even be decorated with a few additions on the edge. As for variations on the rim, on the other hand, one must pay attention to size relationships and arrangement. There are all kinds of possibilities. The three-part division is common. It consists of a main motif, a small second motif, and any added figures. But just a single main motif that decorates two thirds of the rim is very decorative too. And naturally, the thoroughgoing all-around motif can be charming too. Here, to be sure, the sizes of the flowers and leaves should be varied, so as not to look monotonous.

For the "hollow pieces" (pots, cups, vases, etc.), one often decides on a front and a back or selects a complete decor that runs all around the object. If you want to decorate the front and back, then the rule of thumb prevails that the front scene is that shown when the handle in on the right. Here, then, is where one places the main motif. In containers without handles, such as vases, bowls, etc., one may choose as the front a place where, for example, a flaw is to be concealed or a seam caused by manufacture can be seen. The main motif itself should create a certain excitement, being most interesting and relaxed by secondary or scattered figures. Illustrations 46 and 47 show examples of this.

The composition of flower bouquets is also done according to certain rules. In the center we place one (or two to five on larger objects) main flower. Around this we arrange the so-called "linking flowers," which should be somewhat smaller. To finish the decoration, we add lines of small flowers arranged one after the other.

The arrangement itself must be suited to the object in question, meaning that, for example, a tall slim vase requires a bouquet that "stretches" upward. We call this oval standing (Ill. 38, 39,

44). A shallow bowl, on the other hand, requires an oval lying.

One can also decorate a piece completely with small "scattered" flowers, which can be applied almost in a regular order. On the other hand, for landscapes, portraits, still-lifes, etc., one almost always chooses the center of the object or of the bottom. Rims and angles are decorated with gold. With the Indian or Chinese elements of Far Eastern motifs, the composition is usually not left up to the painter, as graphic patterns are used and are almost always applied symmetrically. In addition, they are usually applied with stencils, so that the painter does not need to paint freely. Naturally, one can also develop free designs here too, usually based on existing patterns.

14-15 Loosening-up practice should create completely free and unforced lines that make the wrist loose.

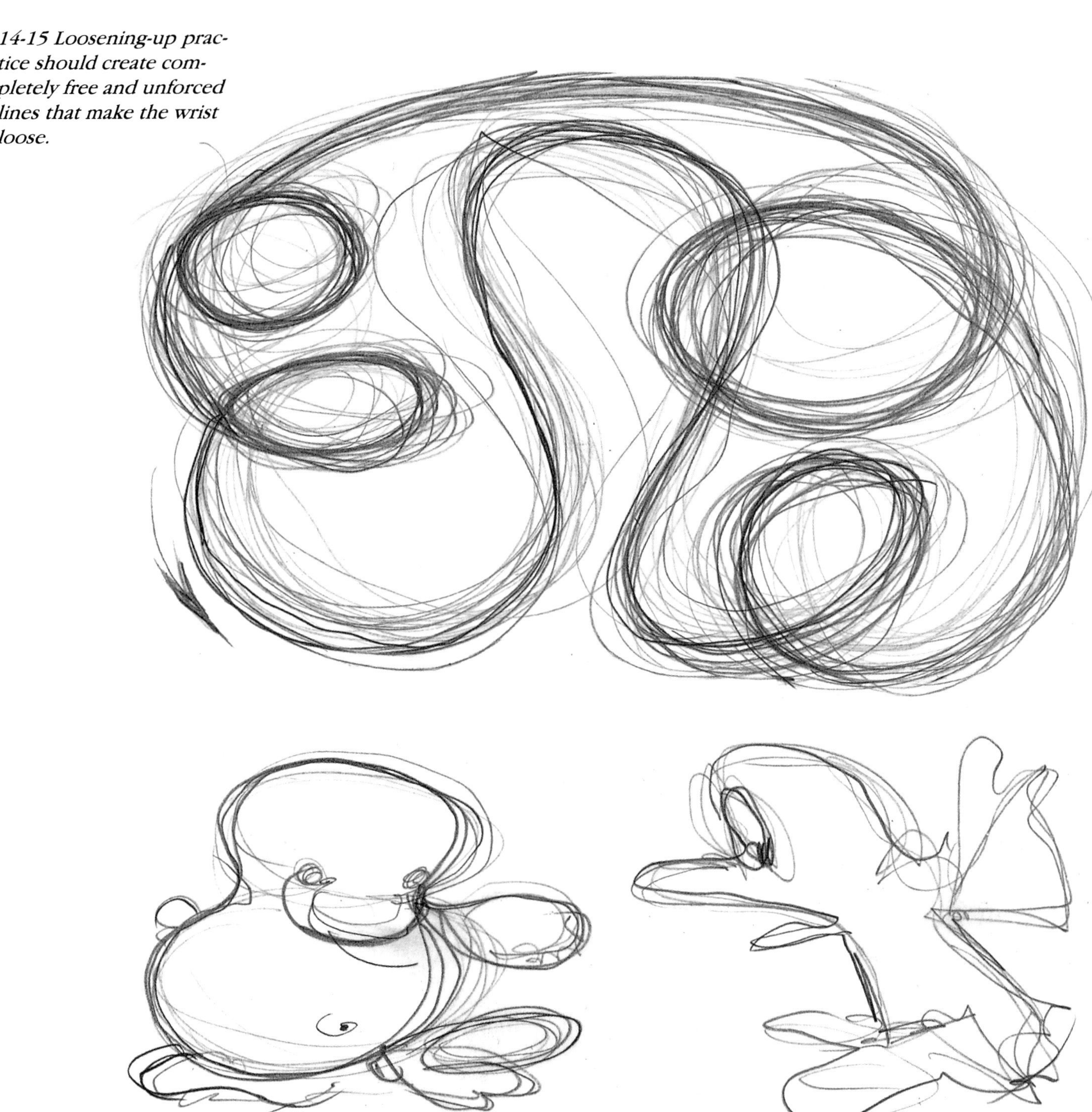

Preparing the Paint

Mixing the paint is not difficult, but one must remember the varying pigment and oil proportions, depending on the type of painting. If the paint is to be kept in a hole palette, it should be mixed not only with thick and thin oil, but also with two or three drops of oil of cloves, in order to keep it usable for a long time. Then it is sufficient to stir the paint in a cup before one starts to paint, and it will be usable all day. For the hole palette, it needs to be mixed only once.

The situation is different when one uses glass palettes, each of which holds only one color. On account of the large surface exposure to the air on these palettes, the paint gradually dries and thickens. Then it has to be mixed anew (about every half hour).

But now to the actual mixing or stirring, as it is also called. According to what is needed for the motif or the number of pieces to be painted, one puts powdered pigment onto the glass plate with the point of the spatula. In the middle of the small pile, a small crater is created, into which one now puts five or six drops of thick oil. Stir lightly in the process, but remember that the number of drops of oil increases with the quantity of powdered pigment. It is always important that the end result should be a creamy paint that just drips from the spatula. Now one adds the thin turpentine to the thick oil, and just enough so that the outer rim of the pile of pigment still remains dry. Now the mixing can begin. This is done by pressing steadily on the mixture with the spatula and pulling at the same time. Then turn the spatula, push the spread-out pigment back together, and flatten it out. Thus the pigment and the oil unite to form the desired paint. If the paint should become too thin, add a little more powder; if it is too thick, add a drop of turpentine. For keeping it in usable condition in the hole palette, as stated before, add two or three drops of oil of cloves. Not more! Many pigments are somewhat coarse and grainy, and thus must be worked with the spatula for a long time.

If you use already prepared paints from tubes or tins, follow the instructions that come with them.

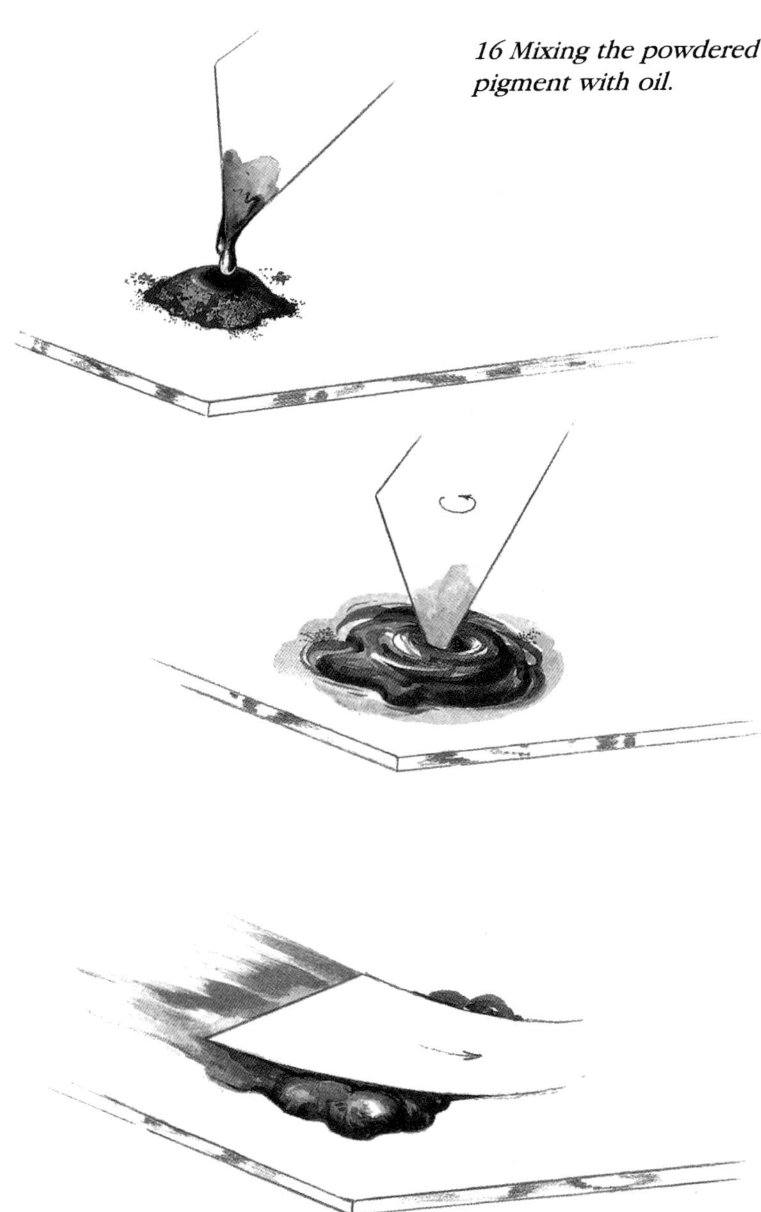

16 Mixing the powdered pigment with oil.

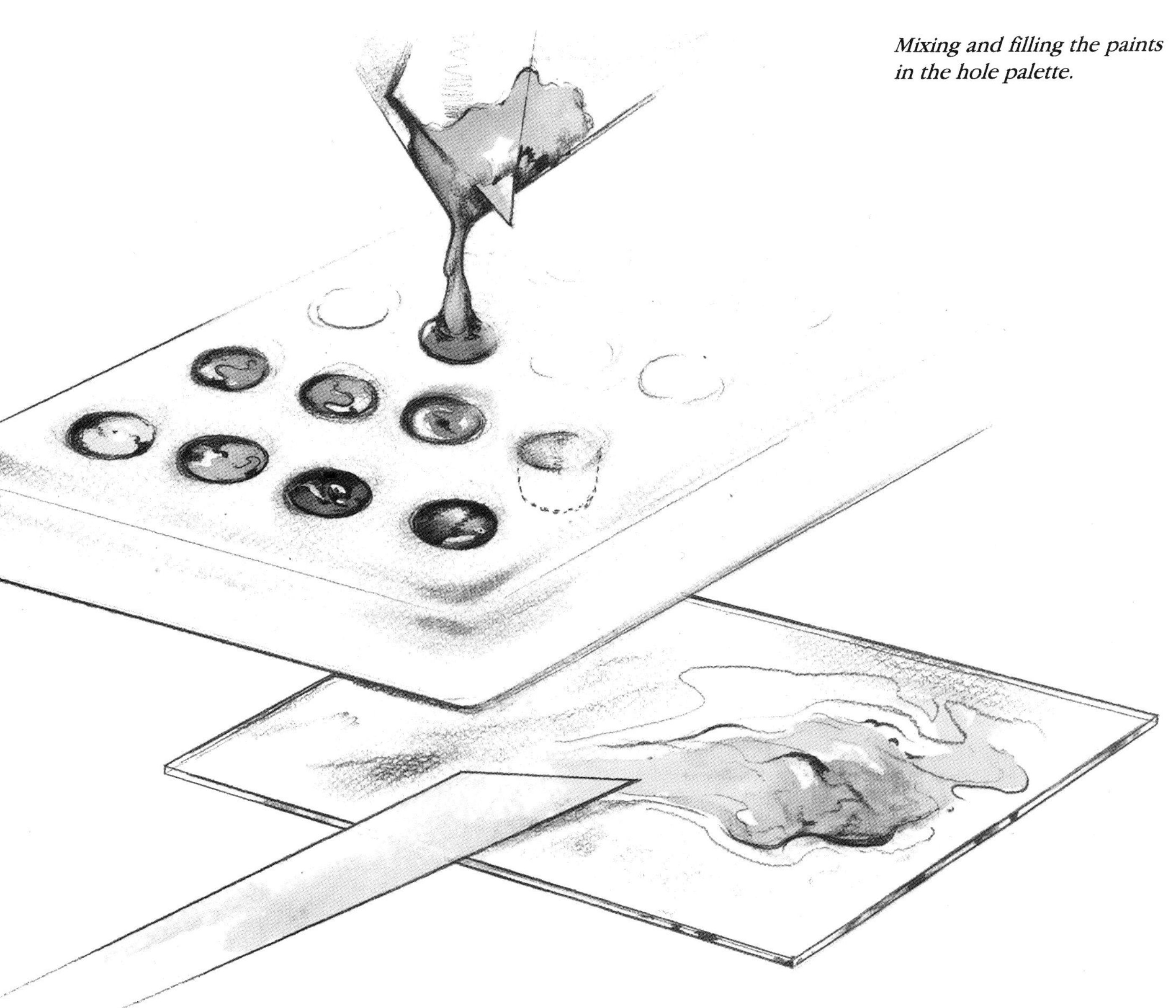

Mixing and filling the paints in the hole palette.

FLOWER PAINTING

Nature Studies

To gain a thorough knowledge of true-to-nature painting, it is almost obligatory to work with the flowers in the garden. A wealth of knowledge of their form, blossom and leaf structure, thousands of colors, incredible richness of types and varieties of flowers, is a great treasure for the incipient porcelain painter. Only after one has made extensive studies does one absorb the many rules of their growth and nature, which one can always turn to.

The flower in a porcelain painting is not always an exact copy of the original in the world of nature, but the basic structures are the same. That means that most of them have actually been "idealized," simply for the purpose of making them suitable for decoration of porcelain objects. A certain stiffness and sometimes a little awkwardness have been taken from them in order to give them more spirit and grace and make them more decorative.

These studies should be conducted in peace and quiet. What kind of flowers you choose for study is completely up to you. It is only important that you provide the necessary patience, for many a flower demands a great deal of time. Just think of the manifold varieties of lilies that exist. But when you proceed systematically and try to acquaint yourself with the plant from the ground up, you will soon realize that your joy in the subject increases, and when you get to know the plant in all its characteristics, you will soon succeed in producing your first beautiful painting.

One begins by drawing the basic shapes of the flowers, in large scale and corresponding to the various actual sizes (Ill. 19). More details can be added when the design includes the blossom, stem and leaves. Let us begin with the blossom. Count just how many individual petals surround the calyx and note how they are arranged. First draw them in crudely, and then define the precise form of every single petal! Then determine the exact downward course of the stem. In the process, note how the leaves grow on the stem and what shapes they have. This initial form of the study should be undertaken with as many different types of flowers as possible. Every type has its own particular shapes, which need to be identified. When these are drawn, paint the surfaces in a quiet color. Here one can already achieve a little plasticity if one can portray light and shadow easily. Naturally, all of this is still being done on paper. Painting on porcelain demands a very different technique, and we want to begin by getting to know the flowers. After this gentle application of the colors (naturally, one can use just one color in the beginning), one adds the details. Always begin with the blossom. Then in the later steps, you have the advantage of not having the green too dominant. In the end, the blossom should be the object that defines the picture to the viewer. In almost every flower, the structural lines of the petals run from their outer edges toward the calyx, where the individual petals come together. This point should always be determined as a kind of orientation. Since this is the same in many different kinds of flowers, it is a big help for the beginner. One need only think

18 Grapes and other fruit studies can be made best with water colors.

19 A variety of flower studies. They should portray as great a variety as possible, since they can also be shown to customers as patterns.

of asters, daisies, anemones, or narcissus. The lines of the petals always run to the point where the flower is attached to the stem.

Now we add the green leaves, very softly and tenderly. Only the central and side veins can be seen at this point. Try to work precisely and conscientiously, so that you can make a truly accurate reproduction of how such a stem and a flower are grown together. How you proceed to work out the individual segments of the drawing is up to you. You can draw in the shadows in something similar to copperplate technique or create quiet surfaces with broad strokes. Be careful to work out carefully, and later on the porcelain, three levels of brightness: bright, medium, and dark tones. These three will do the job completely without adding any great confusion to the motif.

In these nature studies, you are naturally not limited to flowers. Paint anything from nature that pleases you and gives you joy: leaves of trees, small animals, stones, fruits and nuts such as chestnuts, mushrooms, etc. But always stay true to the basic principle of never painting from photographs. If you did, you would be given a prearranged motif that would prevent you from getting to know the subject yourself. One must be able to comprehend the flower, and perhaps also get to know a leaf, in order to see what fascinating secrets the world of nature contains. A printed picture simply cannot provide that. When one takes a razor blade and a loupe and sets out to learn from the ground up how flowers grow, one gains a wealth of experience that is invaluable to the flower painter.

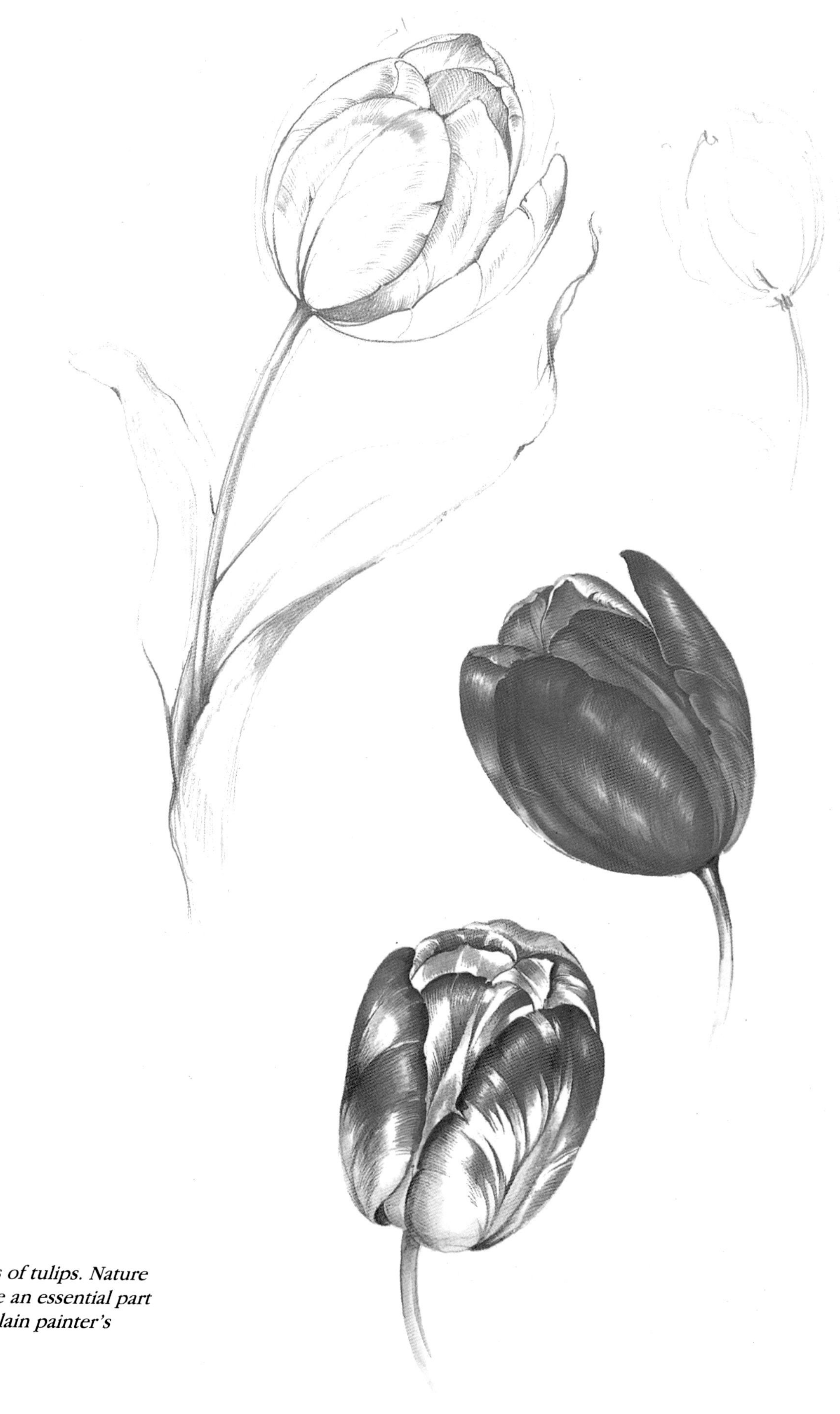

20 Studies of tulips. Nature studies are an essential part of a porcelain painter's work.

21 A watercolor study of the violet poppy.

22 Rose studies from nature.

Rose Painting

The typical porcelain rose is often compared to a cabbage head in terms of its shape. But this does not at all change the fact that the rose in this form has been one of the most popular decorations in porcelain painting for hundreds of years. There is scarcely a porcelain collection, a museum of ceramics, a private collection of plates, or a porcelain dealer's shop window where this motif is not found, either as the only decor or in combination with other flowers in a bouquet. The fact that it is so popular is surely related to its meaning as a symbol of love and its beauty in and of itself.

23 A lavish bouquet of roses in purple, especially suitable for large wall plates or vases.

For our purpose of learning porcelain painting, the rose is therefore very important, because it embodies all the techniques that are needed for painting other flowers as well.

It is also particularly suited to teaching the beginner the main manners of painting flowers.

Rose painting, like that of almost all other flower motifs, is done in three work processes:
—Laying out
—Working out
—Shadowing or detailing.
Please see Illustration 24 first to note these.

24 The familiar porcelain rose, step by step (see opposite page for description of work processes).

For this painting we need the following colors:
—Light purple for the layout
—Yellow-green for the layout
—Dark purple for working out
—Black for detailing the green
—Dark green for touching up the green.

The brush sizes needed for this must be chosen according to the size of the motif. For a flower diameter of about 4 centimeters, the brush used for laying out and detailing the blossom should be 4 millimeters. For drawing, on the other hand, use a 2 mm brush with a good point.

After we have handled and prepared the paint and the piece as already described, we can now finally begin our attempt. Draw the center of the rose with the crayon as a simple circle at first. Try several objects at the same time at first, in order to get a sufficient amount of practice. Now proceed exactly as shown in Illustration 24.

a. Make the first brush strokes with a light shade of purple, extending the brush in half-circles and working toward the right.

b. Take more paint onto the brush (somewhat more on the left side!), and indicate the shadowed leaves with two broad, firm strokes.

c. Take more paint and indicate the heart of the flower in a dark shade.

d. Wash out the brush in turpentine, and use a clean brush to draw out the still-fresh paint of the flower center.

e. Finish the rose completely.

f. Lay out the center, the two upper petals, then paint in the two outermost edges and then join them gently to the center.

g. Lay out the lower petals as indicated by the arrows.

h. Draw in the entire rose in green, putting on the green evenly and softly, and let the layout dry thoroughly!

i. Draw in the rose with a thin brush and dark purple paint, and apply black to the green as well, as on the model.

j. Shadow the rose with light purple and the green with dark green.

k. Finish the rose, making it look natural.

When you proceed according to this plan, you will surely notice that it requires a lot of practice to be able to show your first satisfactory results. Patience and interest will help you to achieve the goal of good porcelain painting.

Manneristic Painting

Flower painting in general can be divided into two main groups. One is the so-called manneristic painting; the other is naturalistic painting. In manneristic painting, the work processes are carried out in a very definite sequence. Every color is applied independently. The general sequence of work is as already described: laying out, working out, and shadowing, meaning that every color is applied separately and also worked out individually after drying. We must settle on a total of five different colors for the blossoms and three for the green tones.
Blossom colors: red, purple, violet, blue, yellow.
Green tones: yellow-green, blue-green, olive green.

This means that for manneristic painting we need a total of the following colors:
Red: red (iron red) for layout and working out
Purple: light purple for layout and dark purple for working out
Violet: same as purple
Blue: same as purple
Yellow: intense yellow (sun or lemon yellow) for layout and a medium gray for working out. Also, for variations in the stamens, a dark yellow, and a powerful brown:
Yellow-green
Blue-green
Olive green
Black
Dark green.

This makes a total of sixteen colors. In manneristic painting, each color is usually kept individually on a glass palette, since one always has just one color to apply.

Manneristic painting took its name from the technique involved, because all the work processes are carried out in a definite sequence or manner.

In what follows, I would like to offer you a brief cross-section of the chief flower motifs used in porcelain painting, in order to explain how they are painted and what techniques are used.

Asters

The aster is, without a doubt, one of the most decorative flowers for porcelain painting, although in a purely technical sense it is very difficult to paint. Please be guided by Illustration 27.

a. Draw a crude outline and the flower structure.

b. After drawing the individual petals of the flower, do the layout with light violet, working in the direction of the center. It is important to avoid making the outer rim of the blossom look like a "cogwheel," and rather constructing an interesting contour (short-long, thin-thick).

c. While the layout is drying, use the washed-out brush to extend a second, bright wreath of the flower and lay out its dark yellow center.

d. Using dark violet, begin to work out the shadowing of the flower, working toward the center as before. Indicate shadows under the circle of light, and lightly work out the center.

e. Draw in the outer contours of the individual petals, bringing out the lights and shadows, likewise apply the green gently and mark it with black, apply a green wash after it dries and work out the center with the stamens.

The aster, with its many areas of light and shadow, is ranked among the "technical" flowers. That means that it requires a certain technique to paint, starting with the layout, where light and shadow have to be indicated. The narcissus, on the other hand, is very different. There the entire yellow surface can be applied evenly in one shade, and only when worked out do the shapes and perspectives come out. You will see examples of other flowers and their portrayal in Illustrations 28 to 33.

One more tip, so as to avoid too much confusion of light and shadow: In every motif, always determine which is the light side and which the shadowed one. When you know from where the light (purely theoretically) comes, it will be considerably easier to locate the shadows correctly in a motif. An old rule says that the light should always come from the upper left, in order to provide a clear orientation. You will also be able to observe that in the pictures in this book. More will be said about handling light and shadow in *Bouquet and Greenery Painting.*

Hedge roses

In the case of the hedge rose, it is important that it be made very delicate and soft, so it will look airy and transparent. One can paint individual hedge roses on small objects such as small bowls, vases, and the like but they can also be included in bouquets on wall platters and tableware. For the learner, their technique is also very interesting since the anemone, ranunculus, and fire poppy are painted in the same manner. They all share a quiet, tender layout and a working out oriented to the direction of growth.

25 Sketches of hedge roses can be made on paper at first.

The colors needed:
Purple, light and dark
Yellow, light and dark
Yellow-green and dark green
Black
Gray and brown.

Illustration 26 shows the work processes.

a. Draw the contours and indicate the direction of growth.

b. With light purple, lay out the outer limits of the petals pointing outward, and use the soft yellow in the direction of the center, use rather greasy paint (thick oil), and let the paint dry away from dust!

c. Lay out the circle of stamens in dark yellow.

d. With dark purple, work out the details, making the strokes run in the direction of the center, make the light areas brighter, and work out coverings and contours to the outer rims of the petals.

e. Apply the green gently and evenly, work out the stamens in brown, and add the shadowings to the blossom in gray, plus the green lines and wash.

For this flower too, it is rewarding to paint several at the same time, thus practicing a large number at once. Every flower naturally turns out somewhat better the more often one has painted that type. The hedge rose is a favorable motif that enjoys great popularity among porcelain painters.

26 The individual steps in painting a hedge rose.

27 One of the hardest flowers to paint: the aster.

28 Studies for a field poppy.

29 An anemone as painted in the styles of three different eras:
a. Copperplate technique, as painted circa 1740 (old, dry porcelain painting).
b. This light and airy style decorates many Art Nouveau porcelain pieces.
c. The lively painting style of today.

30 Naturalistic flower painting, using the gentian as a model:
a. Drawing
b. Layout
c. Finished

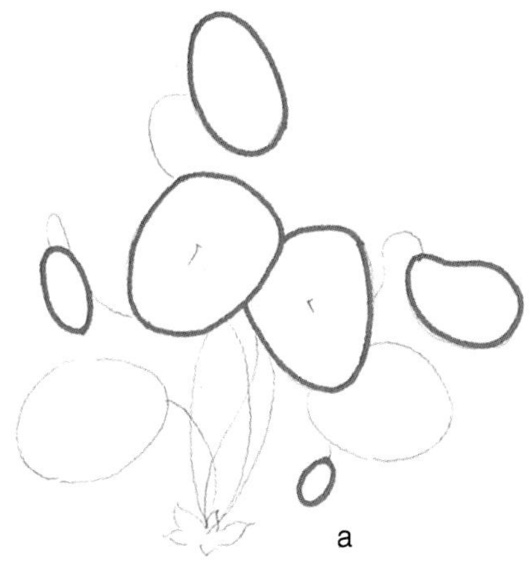

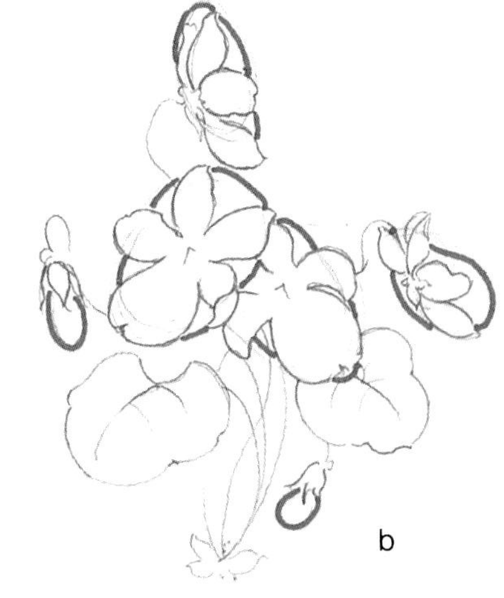

31 The Violet
a. Crude drawing with placing of most important shapes
b. Exact outline of petal and leaf shapes plus stems
c. Adding color to the drawing
d. Working out the violet and green areas
e. Shadowing and adding details (stamens)

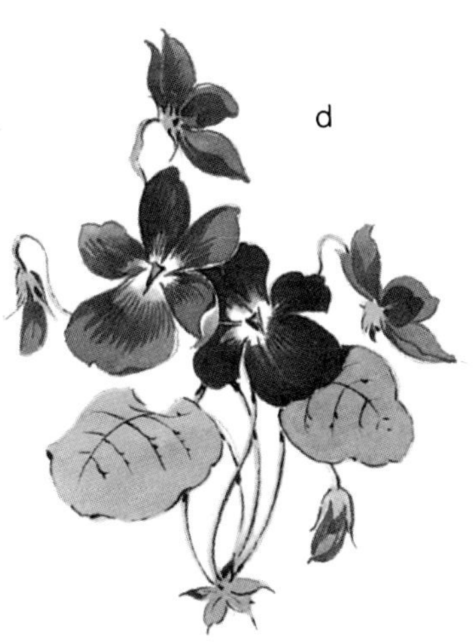

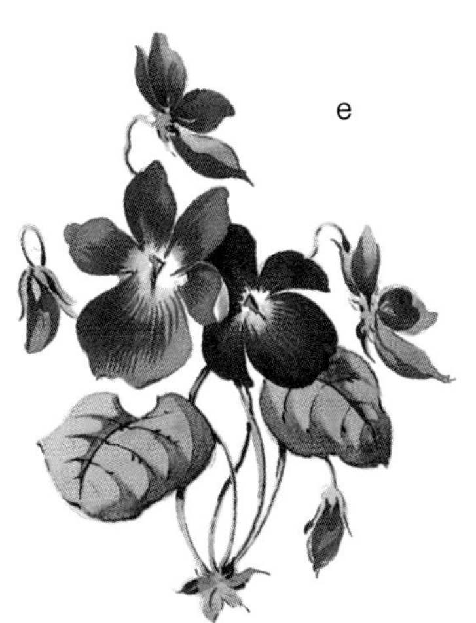

32-33 The process of painting various flowers in three steps each. The arrows show the direction of the brush strokes.
Page : Narcissus, morning glory, zinnia.
Page : Feather poppy, crocus, anemone.
a. Crayon drawing
b. Gentle addition of colors
c. Finishing and adding details.

33 ▷
a
b
c
a
b
c
a
b
c

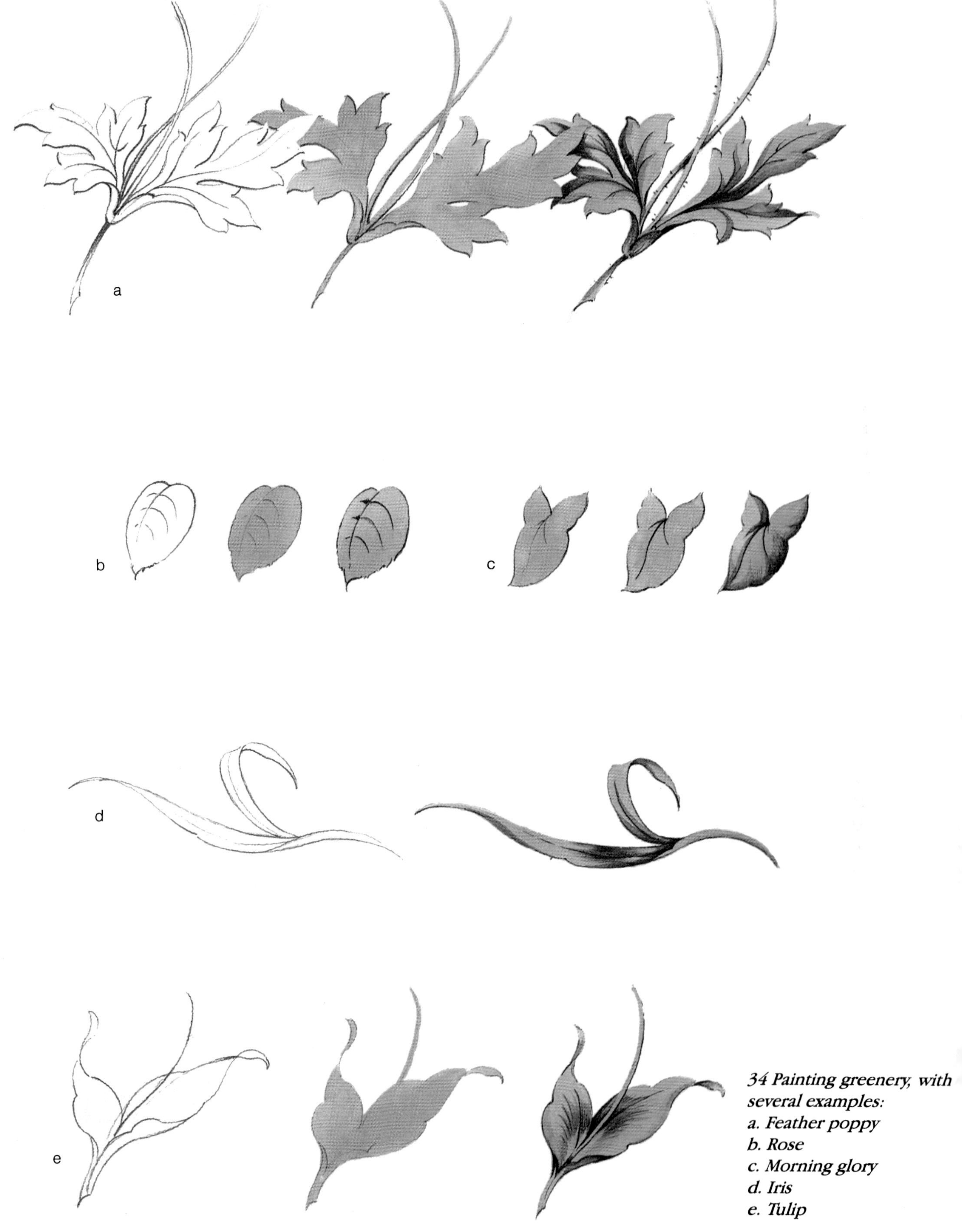

34 Painting greenery, with several examples:
a. Feather poppy
b. Rose
c. Morning glory
d. Iris
e. Tulip

35 A bouquet motif on a cup, with two scattered flowers on the back.

36 A similar decor on a saucer.

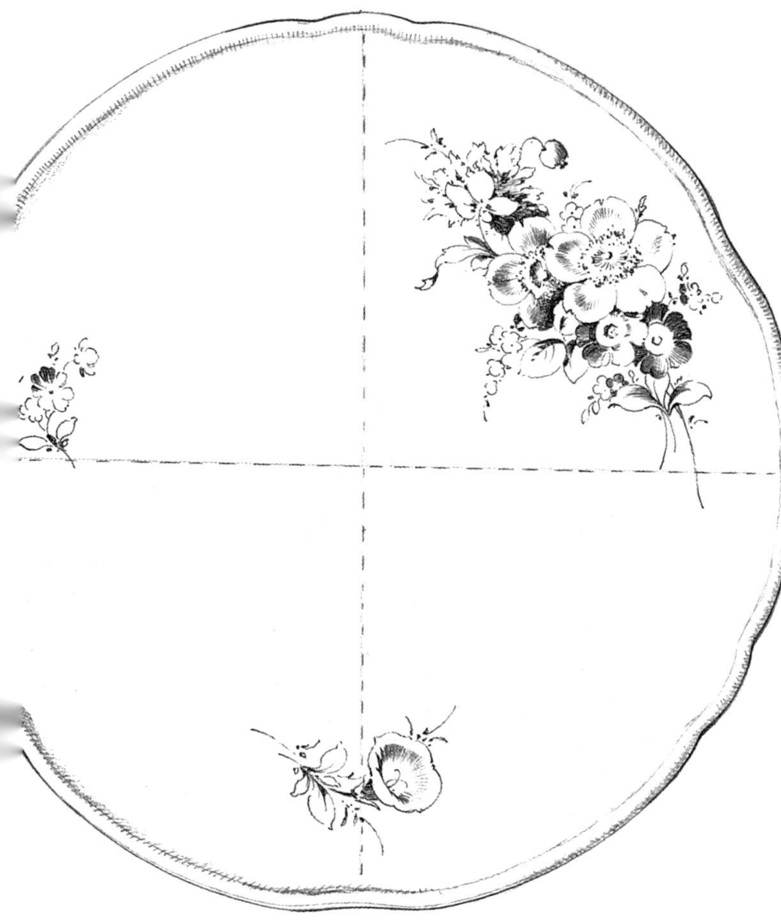

Bouquet Painting and Green Application

In bouquet painting, the direction of the light is especially important, since one can lose one's "orientation" here all too easily, and the whole thing can end up as a mixed-up mess.

All in all, the fanciest bouquets are among the most difficult motifs in terms of composition and light-shadow effects. When you begin, place one or two (no more at this point) in the middle, and arrange the smaller flowers around them. When you have composed several of these motifs successfully, then you can move on to your own combinations, but when you are learning, a basic arrangement is always advisable, one in which the individual flowers can be varied or substituted. Illustration 41 offers examples of this.

A few more tips on handling the green. As already noted, we limit ourselves to three different greens, and even these require a certain regulation. So as not to confuse things too much, and not to have all the yellow-green on the left and all the blue-green on the right side of the bouquet, we make sure that the red and yellow flowers have blue-green stems, and we use yellow-green for the violet, purple and blue ones. You will find this standard applied to many motifs in porcelain painting when you look at the shop windows or catalogs of the well-known porcelain makers. To be sure, this applies only when numerous flowers appear in one motif. If the flower stands alone, naturally yellow-green should be used. In a bouquet, make sure also that the leaves are evenly located, fitting into the spaces between the flowers. The more delicate stems and the smallest twigs of the flowers should be worked out in the remaining olive green.

All the green tones will be marked with black, into which one can mix some green so that it does not look too heavy. Here too it must be remembered that light can come from only one side, so that stems, for example, should be marked only on one side. Then the central and lateral ribs can be applied. The exact process can be seen in Illustration 34. In your nature studies, also determine the exact forms of the individual green of every leaf. Here too, every plant has its own typical appearance, although many are similar, such as, for example, iris green and narcissus green.

37 △

38 △

37 So-called "hanging flower painting" on a teapot.

38 An oval standing bouquet.

39 △

40 △

39 Oval standing flower painting.

40 A round standing rose.

41 A wall-plate bouquet with wild flowers.

When the green paint has dried well, we can begin the green wash, meaning nothing else but giving the leaves the required plasticity. Here too, pay attention to the direction from which the light comes. Arrange the shadowings accordingly. In a bouquet, where one flower overshadows another, a flower can naturally disappear completely into the shadows. Then it really has to be worked out very dark, but without making it look dead. So do not work it out so dark that it is only a spot of color of even intensity with no plasticity. You will find several examples of this in this book, and they will show you how dark a flower in shadow may be and still be a part of a bouquet; see Illustrations 41-44.

Always give the flowers, leaves, stems, and grasses in flower painting the so-called S-curve; which means they should not appear too stiff or have too dominant stems, which can make a painting look lifeless and unappealing all too easily. Therefore we must sometimes idealize some of the flowers that we see in nature. In doing so we take the stiffness that occurs in nature—that of a stem, for example—out of the motif and swing the motion in a large-scale S-curve in the painting (Ill. 44). You will notice that this provides many flowers with a quite magical elegance.

Naturally, this does not apply to naturalistic painting, since here nature should be duplicated unchanged and true to life.

42 A bouquet in typical manneristic style. Note the division of colors, about 2/3 petal colors and 1/3 green.

Single-color plate bouquets with gold grasses. The choice of colors can begin with blue or purple and expand from there.

44 A rich flower bouquet, oval standing, on a vase.

Scattered Flowers

Scattered flowers are used both as individual decor and to liven up more elaborate painting. For several hundred years they have been components of porcelain painting, and despite ever-changing directions in style and fashion, they have remained popular to this day.

In the early days of porcelain decoration, they were utilized primarily to conceal blemishes in whiteware, and when one looks at very old pieces of porcelain in various museums, one can see how often crude cracks in the glaze or oxide flecks on the surface were cleverly concealed. I will never forget when, as an apprentice, we studied many old pieces from the famous Dresden collection and were amazed again and again at the clever division of space on the individual pieces. Only later, when we looked closely, did we recognize that for the most part, only bad spots on the dishes had been covered. The procedure was simple. At first one covered all the flaws of the piece, and then one added the rest of the scattered flowers in harmony with those already painted, so that the result was a balanced decoration.

Today this procedure is generally superfluous, since the technical conditions of porcelain production have meanwhile developed so far that flaws in whiteware are quite rare. Thus one can decorate them without thinking of concealing flaws. If flaws should nevertheless appear, one can always locate the first flower on the flaw and go on decorating from there.

The scattered flowers are usually applied in a strictly organized progression and yet project a relatively informal air, since the spaces between them, along with the white of the piece itself, gives the whole thing a very airy atmosphere. And since so many people take pleasure in this decor to this day, we naturally do not want to ignore it.

Painting scattered flowers calls for a high degree of patience and endurance. It is very difficult to describe how they are painted individually, for first of all there is a great variety involved, and secondly, one's individual training (nature study) is considerably important. But in spite of that, here are a few tips and instructions.

First of all, we should keep in mind what scattered flowers actually represent. Observed from a distance, they are merely individual spots of color, apparently thrown together at random.

45 Small flower studies.

This may well give them their charm when one sees a table covered with this decor. But if one observes these little wonders at very close range, one sees very clearly what a lot of effort and care went into every single blossom.

Layout and details use the exact same processes and techniques as with "big" flowers. The only difference is that scattered flowers are supposed to look somewhat brighter and more decorative. They must never look too dominant, too dark or heavy, since they would otherwise be untrue to their role as subsidiary decoration. Never make them too plastic or "finished." All the paints should be pastel colors, lightly applied. They gain their real charm only when they are worked out, which likewise must be done only sparingly and in the right positions. Let Illustration 48 guide you.

As to the question of arrangement, it can be said that this is really left up to the painter, who can lay out the decor according to his own taste. The usual way is to paint "on holes," in which an outer circle, usually divided into three or five sections, is laid out first, and the additional flowers are added exactly in the centers of the empty spaces in the smaller circle below (Ill. 49). The arrangement on the empty areas of a teapot or plate can be seen in Illustration 47.

46 A large tea can with a loose arrangement of individual small flowers.

47 A classic composition of scattered flowers on a coffeepot.

48 An example of the combined use of scattered flowers and insects (here a butterfly) on one object.

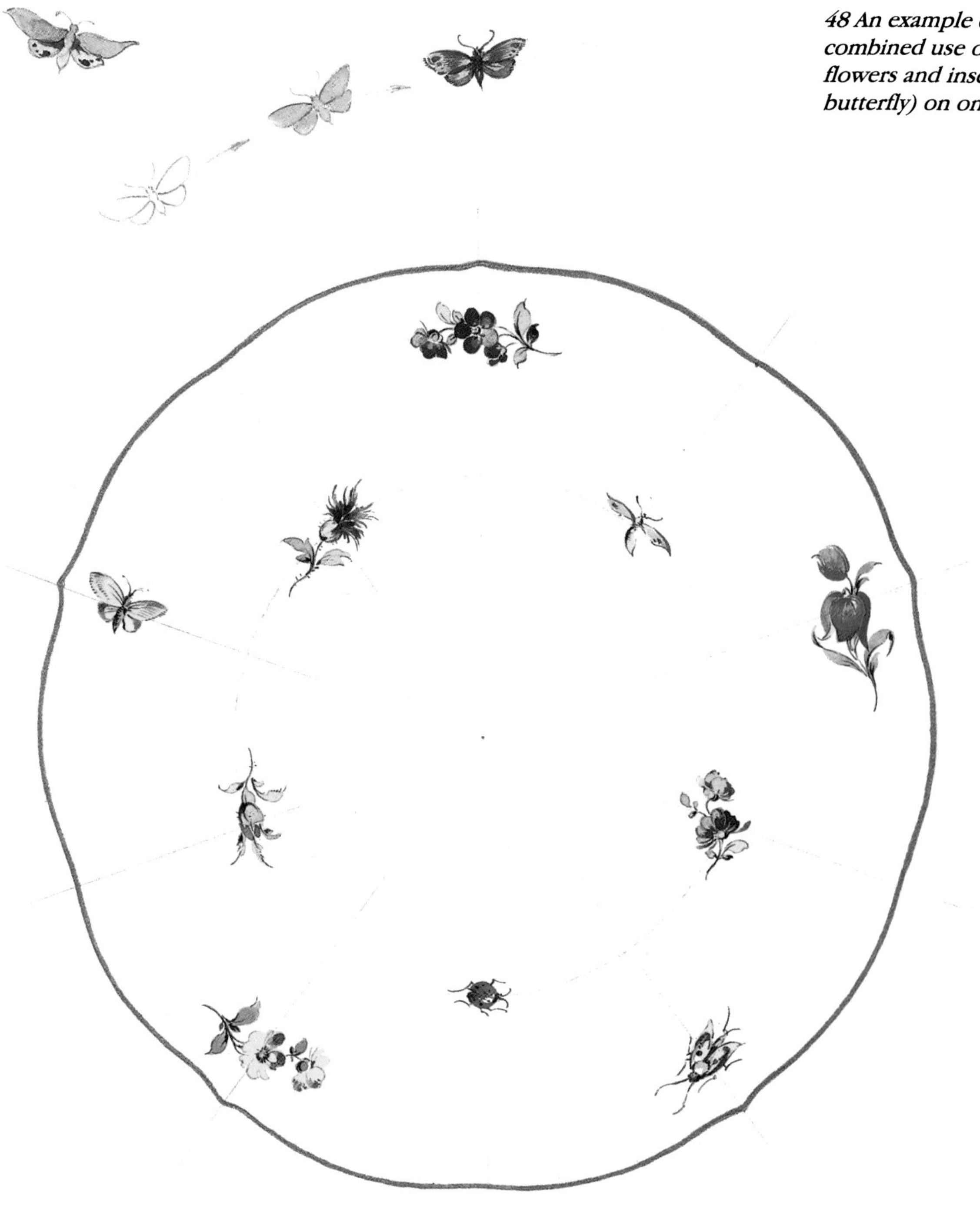

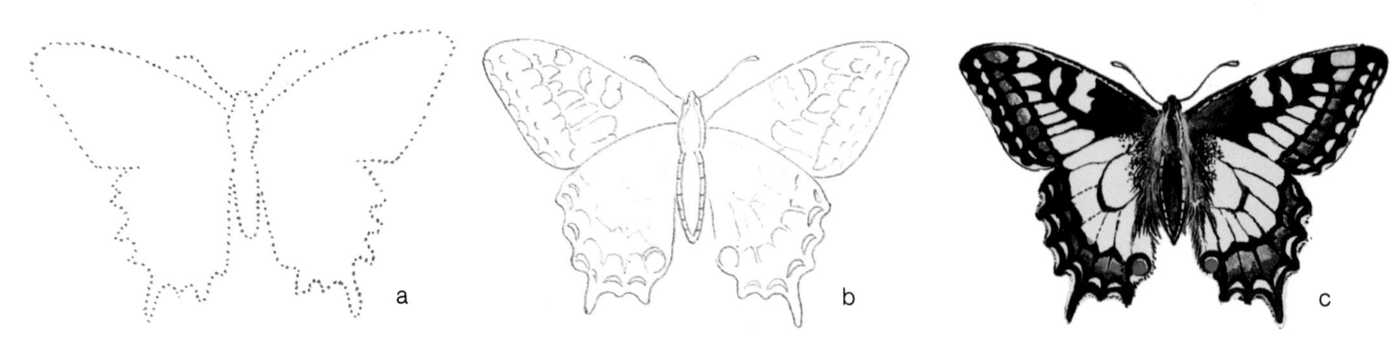

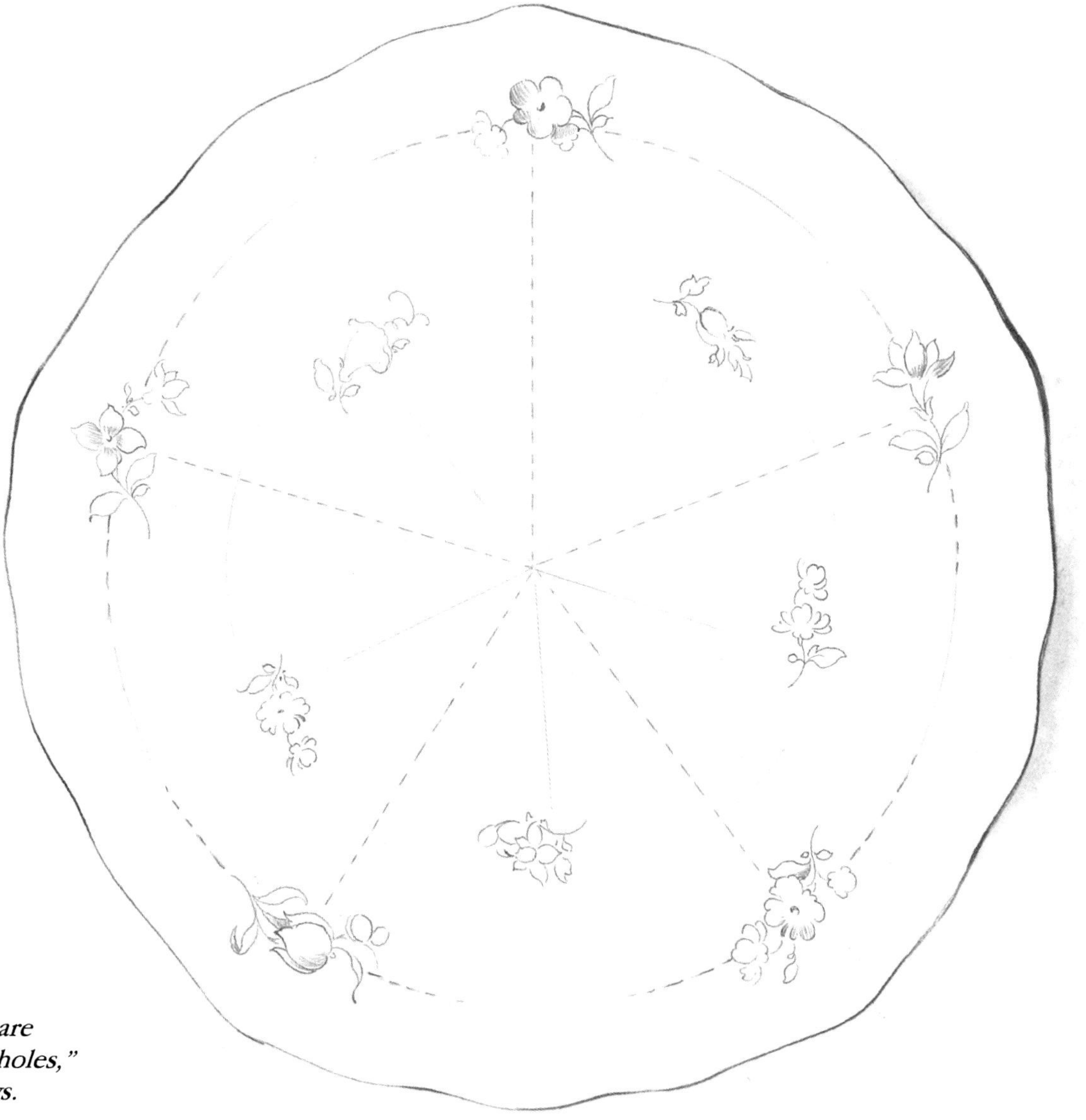

49 Scattered flowers are usually arranged "in holes," as this example shows.

50 Three examples of wreaths of flowers. The sequence of painting steps is shown from left to right each time: outline, layout, working out.

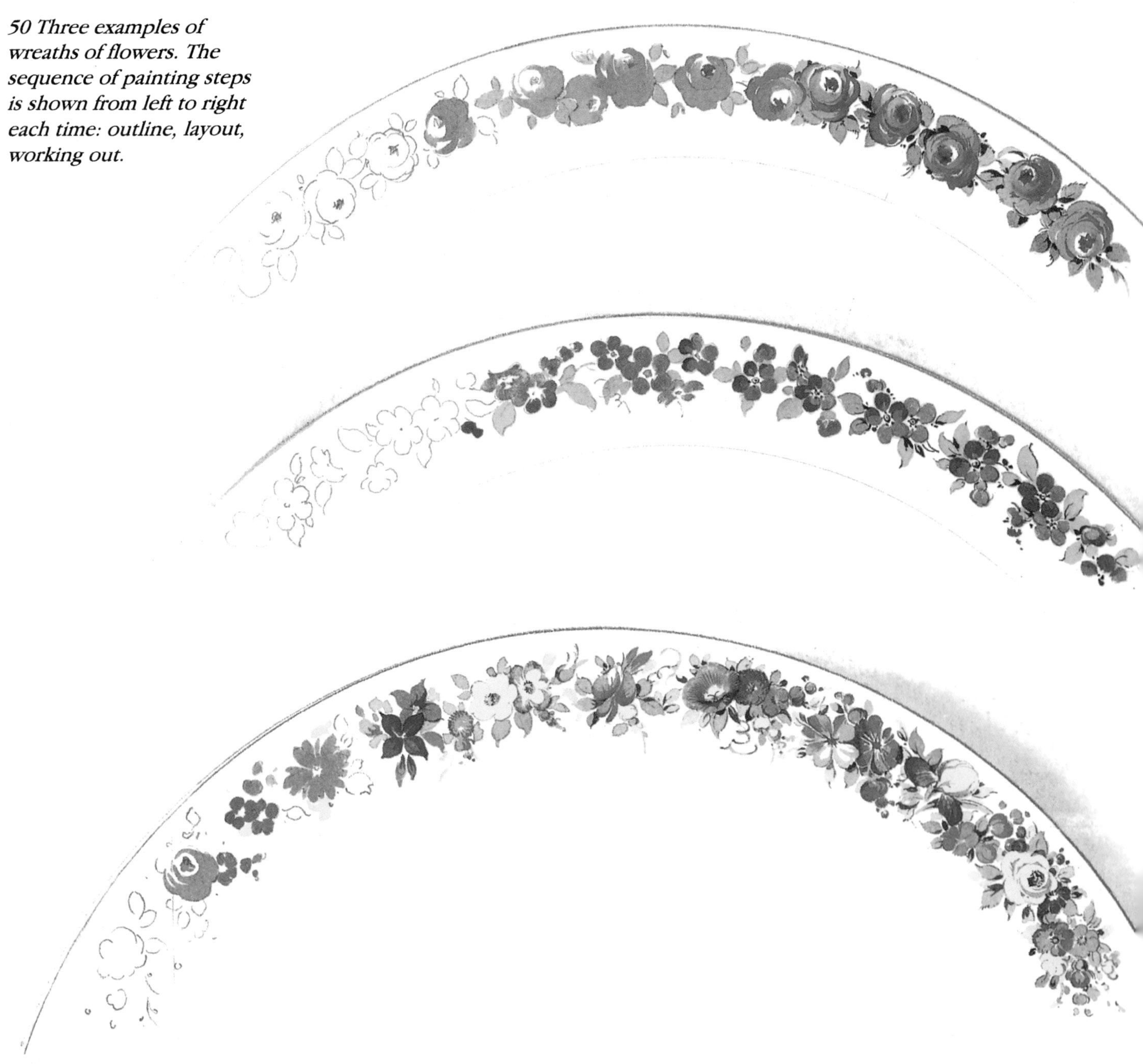

Borders and Tendrils

This widespread kind of decoration provides an ideal extension of scattered-flower painting. In tendrils of blossoms and leaves, scattered flowers are arranged in a loose sequence and thus provide an unforced and informal border decoration. Here too, it is left to the painter whether to do them all in one color or make a wreath of colorful flowers. The blossoms of the forget-me-not and small roses are especially popular for this purpose (Ill. 50).

If one wishes to add something to upgrade the painting, underlaying the flowers with gold or adding decorative ribbons, as we know it from Art Nouveau porcelain painting, can be recommended. It is also important to keep the striping and painting very fine and delicate, for otherwise an overly firm border painting would make the appearance unpleasantly heavy.

The layout and details are done as in the larger motifs. The composition is relatively simple, since the work is almost always done along the rim. Naturally, plates and other flat dishes are particularly suited to it. But a ring of flowers worked into the curves of porcelain articles can also be very decorative. The whole thing can be completed with additions from other motifs, such as small birds, insects or fruits. But this requires far more effort and experience in using the material and should remain reserved for the experienced painter. The types of flowers suitable for this type of decor, where especially delicate and small-growing blossoms should be chosen, include:

Forget-me-nots
Mimosa
Small roses
Starflowers (asteracea)
Bluebells
Larkspurs
Small violet types
Wild vetch.

Any flowered tendril can also be decorated with fine golden grasses, set at harmonious distances between the individual main flowers. To paint them, powdered gold, which is almost 100% gold powder, is suitable. The exact handling of gold is given in the *Gold Decorations* chapter.

Make sure also that the ratio of green leaves does not become too great. About 2/3 flower colors and 1/3 green tones will be best. The green tones are then subdivided into the three main colors already mentioned: yellow-green, blue-green, and olive. When proceeding from the main flowers, paint the buds and small flower twigs gently, working outward. Thus one achieves a good transition to the white of the porcelain.

As already noted, the ring of blossoms should be painted on the outer rim of the piece to be decorated. This includes the outer flange of the plate or the outer rim of the central circle. For the hollow pieces, a so-called bellyband and the upper rim of the vessel can be painted. Individual pieces such as vases, bowls, candlesticks, and even pipe bowls and egg cups, are ideal for this type of decor. For compositions with a golden background, it is advisable to lay out a definite rim extending above and below, so that the band will not go out of control and become wider or narrower. Then too, backgrounds are not limited to gold; a pink or greenish background can also be considered and increase the effectiveness of the row of flowers. Individual suggestions can be found in Illustrations 51-53.

As with all the other decors described here, there are no limits set to the inventiveness and creativity of the painter, and he can vary themes and introduce his own ideas as he chooses.

Compositions with completely different motifs are also possible, for example, with autumn leaves or sea life. Rows of bright-colored autumn leaves or sea shells and other aquatic creatures can produce very beautiful, harmonious rows of decor. Other variations can include:

Rims with wild fruits (blackberries, chestnuts, mushrooms, etc.)
Rims with insects (butterflies, unusual beetles, etc.)
Rims with fruits (strawberries, grapes, raspberries, etc.)
Rims with fantastical flowers (lilacs, forget-me-not, etc.)
Rims with birds and blossoms (pheasants, birds of paradise, orchids)
Rims with sea life (shells, crabs, tropical fish)

When created with precision all of your painted borders will awaken the observer's deep admiration for your artistry.

BACKGROUND FORMATION

The German term *Fond* refers to a plain or even deliberately multicolored background on the white porcelain. It is of particular importance as a background in both still-life and medallion painting.

Quiet Backgrounds for Still-lifes or Portraits

We begin by using the crayon to draw the precise motif on the white piece (flower bouquet, portrait, animal figure, etc.). Then we lay out this main motif as a plain, unified surface with covering paint (Ill. 54a, b).

Next we border the outer rim of the motif or extend the border to the rim of the plate, likewise with covering paint (Ill. 54b). When the paint has dried enough so it no longer sticks to the finger when touched, then formation of the background can begin. With a large brush, preferably of artificial hair (this type does not lose as many hairs and avoids removing lost hairs after the paint dries), the background is now applied in the desired color. Naturally, one should keep the colors of the main motif in mind, so as to achieve as ideal a match as possible. For floral motifs and still-lifes of fruits, the paintings of the old masters of the Netherlands are very instructive, as they generally chose a rather dark background to make the colorful main motif all the more effective. One can select an old wall or a heavy wooden table in order to let the flowers or fruits shine through in all their colorful glory. The application of color must be very lively and even here. Small differences in color, though, are very welcome, since they will liven up the background.

When the painting of the background is finished, we must now divide it up evenly with the stippling, in order to achieve a certain tranquility (Ill. 55a, left).

We always stipple from light to dark, and wipe off the stipple brush now and then with a clean, dust-free cloth, so as not to mix the colors.

When the applied paint is almost dry, it is time to remove the covering paint, which has now stiffened to a unified sheet, with tweezers. Now the white motif comes into view. This now forms the border for our bouquet or portrait (Ill. 55a above and 55b).

For the outer limit at the rim of the plate, a decorative gold line or even a heavier gold band is very suitable.

Blanking Medallion Surfaces

The technique is the same, and the work processes are also the same as before. The main difference is merely that now we do not form the background of the motif in color, but, as Illustrations 51 and 53 show, set the motif on a white surface and apply the colored framework farther out on the rim of the object.

More precise directions, using the example of a round jewelry box:

First delineate that area on the lid of the box that will remain as the white surface for the motif (outline precisely with crayon). Then cover this delineated white surface with covering paint (and if necessary, also define the border of the lid with paint).

The remaining white surface of the porcelain should now be painted in the desired color, then stippled (choose the size of the stipple brush according to the amount of surface).

After a brief drying period, remove the covering paint with tweezers.

The white background area thus obtained can now be decorated with designs of your choice, as you see fit. In order to make the transition from the stippling to white or painted surfaces not to appear too sharp, a thin gold strip or a richer gold band, which elegantly divides the tint of the painted area from the white, is recommended.

A few general notes on handling the background: When large surfaces are to be stippled in a single color, we must naturally beware of the dust that falls on them. A well-cleaned porcelain surface is important, as is the right ratio of oil to pigment. Add a few drops of oil of cloves to the mass of pigment, so it will remain fresh longer and still spread (work) evenly while drying, thus resulting more readily in a truly tranquil colored background. A quiet, dust-free place is naturally ideal for the drying process, particularly so that large surfaces can dry in peace. If a few particles should be caught in the paint all the same, they are easily removed later with the palette knife.

To attain a sufficient glossiness in the colored surface, especially when it should appear very soft and light, it is best to add some flux to the paint. A spatula-tip of it mixed into the pigment powder should be sufficient. But if you need more paint, such as for an entire service, then naturally the portion of flux must be increased accordingly. As a rule, it can be kept in mind that about 1/3 flux should be added (but only to really light colors!).

Other Backgrounds

The background can also be formed in several varying ways. For example, there is the possibility of laying out a colored surface very gently and completely delineated, so you can paint on it later. It is also possible to apply the motif completely at first and then to cover it with paint after one first firing. Both of these variations give the effect of appearing very soft, even clouded, after firing. This surely suits the tastes of many porcelain admirers, who prefer imaginative decors. With expert application, it is even possible to attain a result that resembles the *Pâte-sur-Pâte* technique, a type of porcelain decoration in which the glazed surface shimmers through the thin spots of a flat relief.

51 Colored backgrounds should be used only sparingly in painting.

52 The royal blue cobalt background with a gold rim is especially popular among porcelain painters.

53 A pastel pink background with flower painting in strong colors.

54-55 The formation of a colored background by using covering paint (exact instructions in text).

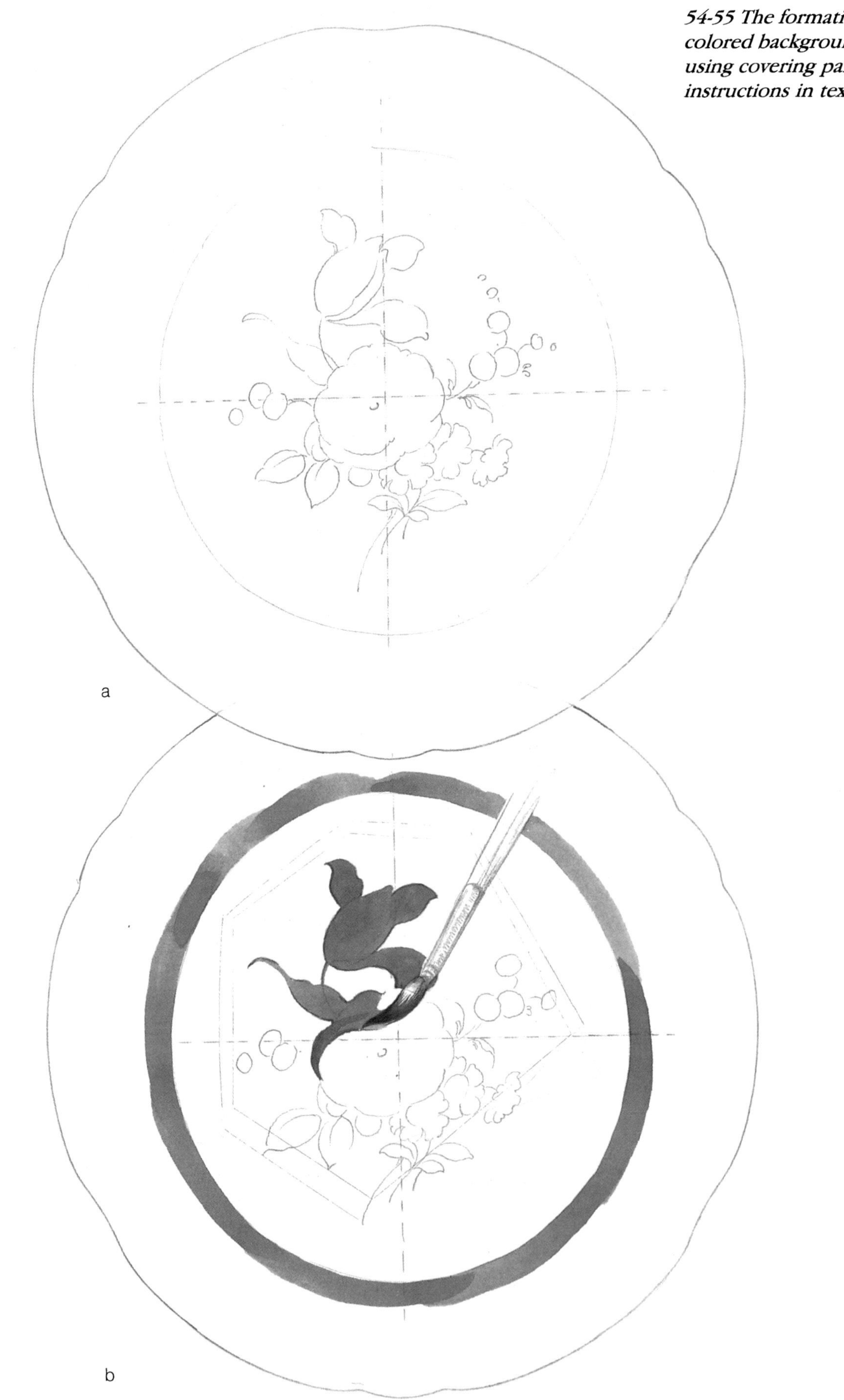

a

55 ▷ b

56 Rich fruit painting in naturalistic style. The process of painting a cherry is shown below.

NATURALISTIC PAINTING

Fruits

In naturalistic painting, everything in all the many motifs that we see every day can be duplicated, everything from still-lifes to portraits to animals and landscapes. The difficulties are really in the technique of painting itself. All the colors are painted wet on wet, and with even the first strokes, one must have the finished picture in mind; the painter must see with his mind's eye just exactly how it will look when it is finished.

Probably the greatest unknown variable will be the behavior of the paints, which come into contact with countless possible mixing conditions, during the firing. Although almost all paints will mix with each other, there are still important possibilities, based on experience, that must be kept in mind. A well-known problem is caused by the use of yellow and red together. In a whole row of fruits it is simply impossible not to have to mix them (especially for peaches, nectarines, apples and pineapple). The more often one tries to bring these two colors into harmony with each other, the better the routine and assurance pay off in the end product.

But the nature studies already discussed also form an important part in the handling of this technique. It is obvious that every flower, every fruit, and every portrait comes out all the better according to the extent to which it is studied and worked out. This at the same time means that the painter must decide how far he can take his personal qualifications. Several hundred studies, plus the ability to keep going despite unsuccessful attempts, are necessary. The watercolor technique bears only some resemblance to that of porcelain painting. A watercolor dries onto the paper, while a painted piece of porcelain still has to allow the process of the paint melting over it during firing in order to appear in all its glory. That means there are many colors and individual tones that considerably change their appearance during firing. To take note of this and anticipate it is one of the essential abilities of a good porcelain painter. Here again, the knowledge gained through many attempts is necessary.

The newcomer should calmly get thoroughly acquainted with the palette of colors chosen by him and test them in a multitude of variations. Mixing the most varying tones results in a mass of precise information on these experiments. But one should pay the strictest attention to make sure that the same firing temperature is always maintained in the same firing conditions (see *Firing Painted Porcelain*).

When mixing problems must be worked out, it is helpful to bring different colors gently into contact. Begin by mixing or striping the colors together, softly and thinly, in order to see how they burn at different consistencies. You will soon ascertain that one can create very soft, gentle-looking transitions without spoiling the colors. For yellow-green transitions in particular there should be no problems, likewise for blue-violet and red-brown combinations. To be sure, mixing red and yellow will cause the porcelain painter to take a little extra care, since these two colors react strongly because of their chemical composition. But if the transition is kept in soft pastel colors, as for a peach, then this too should not cause any great problems (Ill. 56).

For composing naturalistic paintings, of course, the ground rules are a little different from those of manneristic painting. For a bird or landscape painting we cannot choose the same combinations that a bouquet requires. For fruits, to be sure, the arrangement is somewhat the same. Place one or two large fruits in the center of the design, and arrange smaller fruits in other colors around them, finally completing the picture with small twigs and flowers. For example, an apple (red) could be in the center, two plums (blue) flanking it, and small flowers (yellow) for decoration. And don't forget greenery of whatever shades. But make sure that the shade is the appropriate one; for example, don't put cherry-green leaves around a pear.

The number of variations for fruit is every bit as great as for flowers. At the beginning, though, one should always stick to a few basic motifs, until one gets into a certain routine.

The technique of fruit painting is probably the most difficult type of porcelain painting practiced today. All of the many nuances of color that arise when the piece goes into the oven must be planned precisely in advance. Here not only do two colors react with each other, but it happens that up to four or five colors must interact in the firing in order to achieve the desired shade of color. This is especially true of very bright-colored fruits, such as a completely ripe pineapple, where it is extremely difficult to make all the colors harmonize with each other.

For the beginner, I would recommend the following fruits: pears, apples, cherries, and plums. Here too, one must practice until the basics are familiar, in order to go on to more difficult motifs. I would like to expand on this, using the cherry as an example.

—The Cherry (Ill. 56)

a. Draw the exact contour and apply the red tones in the direction of the arrow.

b. Apply the red tones in the direction of growth and open the reflection area.

c. Apply the green softly to its outlined areas (showing movement).

d. Work out the red, showing light and shadowed sides, applying the deepest reds right around the reflection, apply the green as with flowers (but not in black, rather in an earth color, brown, tan, ochre).

How a fruit looks and what characteristics it has are shown best by nature here too. The still-lifes of many earlier painters can serve as models here. After the appropriate practice, try with confidence to paint fruit with a background and use the techniques already noted with covering paint.

If the first attempts do not immediately turn out right, don't give up, but always keep in mind that the masters of olden times also needed a long time before they became masters. In the Albrechtsburg in Meissen there hangs a painting that shows Johann Friedrich Böttger (1682-1719), the inventor of the first European resin porcelain, and his colleagues thoroughly exhausted because yet another attempt had failed.

Naturalistic fruit painting is, of course, painted from the hole palette, since we must have all the colors fresh at hand. We have already discussed how you can keep the paints usable for several days.

But now it is time to discuss the importance of the stipple. A stipple brush is a feather brush cut off at an angle; here too, there are numerous sizes. It is necessary to achieve gentle color transitions, such as exist naturally on fruits. The technique demands caution and fingertip feeling.

57 A study for a wild-fruit painting.

—Stippling

If one wants to have two different colors flow softly into each other, then one uses stippling. First of all, the two colors are carefully brought close together (but not touching!), according to the pattern. On the peach in Illustration 56, for example, they are red and yellow. After brief drying, one carefully stipples the colors together with the stippling angled brush, working from light to darkness, thus from yellow into red. One more or less pulls the colors over each other. But be careful, for the colors must not look pasty sitting one above the other, for during firing the brilliant, glowing colors would be diminished or completely burned away. With red and yellow, as already noted, the danger of being cooked away is especially great. One can stipple other color mixtures for a relatively long time and attain very soft intermediate tones, which is especially important with apples, pears, quinces and also lemons. Care should also be taken that the stipple brush is wiped on a clean cloth now and then during the course of the work, so that bits of paint do not stick in the brush and get applied where they are not wanted. If you have difficulties while stippling, a separate test on a tile or an old dish can be recommended. Firing tests are also necessary in this technique of porcelain painting.

The technique of stippling will also be of use in other types of porcelain painting. We already know it from the background formation and will meet it again when we deal with Indian painting, where the decoration of large surfaces must sometimes be handled (large vases, for example).

58-59 Butterflies and other insects are shown in many publication; one can make good use of them in somewhat simplified form.

Insects

The use of insect motifs is likewise as old as porcelain painting itself. They are to be found on the earliest products of the first European manufacturers, usually in combination with scattered flowers. They are almost always portrayed in stylized form. They have often been made more brightly-colored and imaginative than they occur in nature. In particular, delicate, shimmering wings of small beetles or gnats have been preferred. Thus portrayed, the insects give the impression of a sunny summer meadow in which they swirl around among the individual flowers.

The technique of painting them is relatively simple. We begin by drawing the contours gently with the steel pen and tenderly coloring the resulting surfaces (for pen drawing, see *Indian and Far Eastern Painting*). Their composition corresponds to that of scattered flowers; we simply leave out some of the scattered flowers and put insects in their places. In doing this, it must be remembered always to alternate flowers and insects (Ill. 48).

Butterflies, in all their glorious and varied color, are also very popular in porcelain painting. They do, though, demand a considerably greater amount of work. The details of the wings, often very minuscule, and the range of colors demand patience and stamina of the painter. The layout can be done in two different ways: freehand for the already experienced painter, or with a stencil for the beginners (for stencils, see *Indian Painting*).

For freehand drawing, we begin by making the outlines and contours as precisely as possible with the crayon. After that we paint all the markings and veinings of the wings and body of the butterfly in black. Now an intermediate firing is recommended, to avoid letting the markings dissolve while laying out the surfaces in color. This firing can be relatively low, since it only needs to fix the markings (400-500° C suffice).

Now we can add the colors in peace. Here the tones can be laid on quietly but strongly, since every color will retract somewhat during firing, but the butterflies should radiate strong and satiated colors (Ill. 48).

When drawing from a stencil, only this first work process is different, this being the application of the outlines by tracing. All the further steps remain the same.

Birds

Bird painting has its admirers among hunters and nature lovers in particular. And in fact, a vase decorated with a pheasant or a wall plate with a hunting still-life can be very charming. The choice of motifs is endless here too. The many types of birds that can be portrayed presents us with a simply inexhaustible field of activity. And we do not need to limit ourselves exclusively to native birds. Just think of the colorful "birds of paradise" of Australia and the American peacocks. Or of the toucan or the parrot, which can be portrayed so well along with an orchid plant. Whether on a branch or not, with flowers or with fruit, whether flying or sitting, there are no limits to the motifs. It can be an oriole picking at a grape or a kingfisher catching a fish. The detailed, true-to-life portrayal is naturally important. A bird quickly makes a twisted, wrongly proportioned appearance if it is portrayed wrongly. Here too, of course, one really should begin with nature studies. But naturally it will not be possible for everybody to obtain many stuffed specimens of rare birds to study. Here we can make use of good photographs from nature and animal publications. Whoever has trouble with freehand drawing should use the stencil here too (see *Indian Painting*).

Birds are painted, as a matter of course, from the hole palette, since we have to have all the colors fresh and close at hand and are using a wet-on-wet technique. Single pieces like vases, wall plates, jewelry boxes, wall pictures of several tiles, hunting trophies of porcelain, collection plates, and even pipe bowls are particularly suitable bearers of these motifs. Every devotee of hunting will be pleased by a well-painted bird motif on porcelain.

The process of painting a kingfisher on porcelain will be described below (Ill. 61):

a. Drawing the motif, putting special care into the proportions and relative sizes (length of wing, tail, and body overall), gently indicating what color goes in what place, indicating surroundings such as branches, flowers, fruit or landscape.

b. Gently applying the colors, using wet-on-wet technique, painting as dry (thin oil) as possible, forming feathers softly, blending them together, not yet adding any details (eyes, claws, smaller feathers), adding surroundings such as branches and the like lightly and sketchlike.

60 Before adding the colors, one should first prepare single-color studies in order to get acquainted with anatomy and feather placement.

Now an intermediate firing (400° C) is recommended in order to fix the layout so it will not soften when the rest of the picture is worked out.

c. Now the picture can be worked out in peace. First we draw the most important feathers (wings and tail first, since these feathers show the strictest order most), then the softer down of the chest and back; we can calmly blend the colors into each other to create an impression of softness, and then paint the better-defined features like the beak, eyes and claws, while making sure that everything is located properly! Using the palette knife, feather structures or highlights of the beak and eyes can be added; one must stick precisely to the pattern. The colors should not be made too dark, so that the bird, especially on small porcelain objects, will not look too heavy and dull. Do not hesitate to blend the colors into each other on birds with gentle color transitions, since almost all colors "carry" in firing, firing away is very rare and actually occurs only when the paint has been applied too thickly.

Now for the surrounding field into which the bird motif must fit. Be sure that the surroundings are typical of that bird in every detail. For instance, tropical birds belong with broad-leafed plants and their fruits. Native songbirds, on the other hand, should be shown with any native broadleaf or coniferous trees; birds of prey can be shown hunting along waters or cliffs. Work out the appropriate landscape so that it does not become more important than the bird. Composing it in almost pastel lightness is sufficient.

61 The kingfisher catching a fish—a popular motif on container lids. The steps are described on page 60

a

b

The animal picture, using a cat as a model (exact steps described in text).

c

d

Animal Pictures

For an example of an animal picture, we shall choose the cat as a popular domestic animal. But the technique described as follows is also usable for many other animals.

Begin by choosing the model according to your taste. You can work from a published photo that you like or from personal studies. Again, we will progress in clearly delineated work processes. Start by making a stencil of the picture, if you find a freehand drawing to be too difficult (see *The Stencil*). Illustration 95 shows the precise steps.

a. Stencil or draw the motif on the cleaned piece of porcelain. Be sure to make clear lines and correct proportions, and avoid an overly dark drawing, since this could be a source of trouble later. So make the lines on the object as gentle and light as possible.

b. Now paint the most important contours of the eyes, ears, mouth and other major details in a dark gray (no black). Even now, deliberately leave bright reflections on the nose or eyes in white. Thus you will avoid later corrections or unnecessary scratching at the finished painting. Now also indicate hair patterns or spots with softly broken gray tones. This will make the later precise painting easier for you. At this point an intermediate firing is recommended, so as to burn the paint in at about 600° C and prepare for further depiction of the hair.

c. Now we can add the first color tones of the eyes and hair. Follow the pattern of the photo or drawing of the model and preserve the nuances. Every color should be applied true-to-life. In the example of the cat, this creates no difficulties, for the colors used, such as gray, ochre, green, olive and chestnut cause no problems when mixed. They do not react negatively with each other during firing.

In this third step of the work, the perspective can be added to the picture (ears, hair patterns, etc.). Also add the first fine hairs of the coat. Pay attention to the direction of growth and the structure. In the process, it is a good idea to change brushes to achieve the finest strokes. Choose the thinnest brush you have for this.

d. In the last and likewise the most difficult step, the picture takes on its finished appearance. All the details are added, and the animal portrait takes on its necessary plasticity. Put the hair structures together delicately and pay attention to the precise division of light and shadow. Orient yourself here precisely to the details of the model.

When the structure of the coat is finished, one can also add fine details with a somewhat bigger brush, in order to attain the necessary integration of the entire motif. According to the basic color of the cat's fur, we add the gentle tones, but be sure that the painting has dried well before adding these details.

To finish this work, put in the light-colored whiskers in white. Small reflections of light in the eyes and nose also make the painting more lifelike.

63 Animal pictures usually require thorough studies of the model's anatomy. Here is a horse's head, drawn on paper with a pencil.

Landscape Painting

The landscape motif is preferred when kept inside a frame, usually a gold or colored border. This has the advantage of giving the entire landscape a closed, rounded-off appearance. Since landscape painting is usually used for wall decorations, wall platters or porcelain plates are the ideal places for it. With dishes that include a relief in their structure, a colored bordering is often superfluous, since there is already a frame provided. But landscape painting has also been used on entire table services. At the very beginning of porcelain painting, princes and kings had their favorite castles and pavilions painted by artists. Many of these early examples have been preserved, and it is impressive to see how much delicacy and precision of detail they were given.

How old the tradition of landscape painting is can be seen in the fact that long before the first European hard porcelain had been produced in Meissen, tea shops, mountains, herds of animals and hunting scenes were painted on porcelain in China.

The first such motifs in Europe (ca. 1720) were imposing castles and parks, churches, and cloisters. Later a transition was made to market places, harbor scenes or even everyday scenes of city life. Great enthusiasm for such scenes developed among the masters of oil painting.

It is best to begin with a simple, perhaps even invented landscape. For example, a building, a tree, a scene from a body of water, perhaps a riverbank, and naturally a portion of sky. Whether you also want to venture on to add the portrayal of people to such a scene is left to your ability.

As for the composition of this kind of porcelain painting in color, it may be said that you can work in one color or in several. In the single-color variation, the use of purple in particular is highly popular. It also has the advantage that one can put it on almost complete. For working out the details, just a few concentrated brush strokes are necessary. Let us look first at the work processes of multiple-color painting (Ill. 66).

a. Define the outer frame; working with a colored background is particularly suitable. Draw in the picture precisely (a screen grid can be of use here); if you have chosen an excerpt from a larger picture, make sure that the excerpt amounts to a balanced composition, so that the details of the motif are not all situated in one corner of the frame, leaving empty spaces to dominate in other places. The main motif (church, farmyard, etc.) should be situated a little to the side, toward the frame, and to balance it, on the opposite side there should be some object present (a smaller building, trees, bushes), and as a third focal point, the sky, for example, can be shown as somewhat restless.

64 With a sketch pad in your pocket, a walk can become a study excursion and provide you with suitable motifs.

b. Apply the motif in a bright but lightly plastic manner, begin to suggest light and shadow, then draw in houses and other non-natural components of the motif (ships' masts, fountains, lights, windows, doors, freight for ships or wagons, fences, etc.) with a medium brown shade (Terra di Siena). Then add shores, trees, bushes, sky and water brightly. Make sure that the color shades do not have a harsh, unnatural effect, and now too, apply the green shades naturally. In order to attain convincing earth tones, simply add a little ochre or gray to the green. With a little practice, one can already complete the water and sky in this layout. If you want the sky to look somewhat cloudy and restless, put it on first in stripes of a gray-blue-light brown tone. After a brief drying, wash the brush out in turpentine and bring the white clouds out of the already applied paint. Be sure to give the clouds different shapes and sizes, in order to make the sky as interesting as possible. The situation is similar for the water, except that after laying it on horizontally, light points in the reflecting surface of the water should have the paint removed. If the surface of the water is to look restless, though, we must also add some cloudy effects here, so as to suggest the foam of the waves.

c. Now an intermediate firing (400° C) is recommended for this technique too, in order to protect the layout from softening while being worked out.

Next the precise formation of the motif can begin. We want to begin with the main components such as buildings, ships, wagons, or bridges and whatever architecture remains. This is best done by closing off all clearly recognizable shadowed areas at the beginning. This is especially true of shadows between individual buildings or on their roofs; then follow the walls of the houses and any other larger flat surfaces. Always be determined to match the exact shade of the original, to make your porcelain painting really true to life when it is finished. Now come all the smaller details such as windows, chimneys, utility poles, roof tiles and all the fine points that we find in such a picture. Use quiet dark brown tones for this, in order to make the drawing clearly recognizable as well. Light-reflecting spots can also be taken out with the palette knife now (for example, those of light shining on glass windowpanes, metal parts, precious metals, or reflections from water or wet tree leaves).

The actual nature of shores, cliffs and roadways can now be worked out gently in appropriate earth or green shades. Everything should have a soft, airy effect, and the only strength—in a tree, for example—should proceed from the trunk and branches. The best shades are ochre, cinnamon green, yellow-green, blue-green and various brown tones such as sepia, Terra di Siena, umber and yellow-brown. For the light sides of bushes and trees you can use some light yellow, in order to emphasize the leaves directly in the light. Before you begin your work, look at the portrayal of landscape painting in Illustration 66. You will be able to show the transition with all its details, and the beginner in particular has a guide for the first steps in this area.

The framing of the finished picture can be taken from the *Gold Decoration* section.

In painting a landscape in one color, we must first select the suitable color. As already mentioned, purple enjoys great popularity for this purpose. But versions in cobalt blue and chestnut are often seen too. The layout should be carried out exactly as described in a and b above. The essential difference consists only of the fact that one can paint in more details during the laying out than in the multicolored type, since one must apply only one color. This means that you can already pick out details during the laying out and make them almost complete. As a result, working out the picture requires only individual, deliberate brush strokes to emphasize particular details. Finally it should be said that landscape painting necessitates a good amount of time, stamina, and a considerable degree of devotion on the part of the painter.

Individual Buildings

Many amateur painters paint famous and historical buildings, such as castles, churches, city halls, bridges, and the like on wood, cloth, glass, or paper. Naturally, one can also apply this theme to the realm of porcelain painting.

This time, though, it is not a world-famous structure that shall serve us as a model, but an old half-timbered house. In your neighborhood there is surely a charming object that is worth portraying, whether it is a lovely house, an isolated farmyard, a well-known old tavern, or a city villa from the turn of the century. Naturally, a plate depicting a modern one-family house can also bring joy to its inhabitants.

The process of creating such a picture follows. First select the suitable object for painting. Wall plates or porcelain platters are particularly desirable as bearers of pictures. The latter are also suitable for a frame.

The model (a photo or your own studies) should be as near as possible to the same size as the later picture, since you can thus save yourself the bother of transposing it to the right scale, which can easily lead to untidiness and errors of perspective for the amateur.

a. In this painting technique too, we naturally begin by drawing the most important contours and details. This time, try to do without using a stencil. Buildings are formed mostly of straight lines, which one can also create with a ruler. The exact dimensions can be taken precisely, to the millimeter, from the original design. Details like house numbers and the like can be left out at this stage, since such details just create unnecessary problems now and can be drawn in much more easily later. Plant growth such as trees, shrubs, or bushes can be just suggested schematically, since they have a decorative function and should not distract from the main motif of the house.

b. Next we apply the basic colors of the individual surfaces of the house. Base the color tones on those of the model. Since there are often rather quiet, single-color transitions, mixing is not necessary.

In the individual segments of the facade of a house, the heaviest shadows can now be added (especially in the case of very boxy architecture). This gives an impression of perspective to the entire picture. Smaller shadows of chimneys or cornices can also be lightly suggested.

The green areas should now be initiated sparingly, since these surfaces will be distracting otherwise. Apply the appropriate shade of green softly with several levels of depth; this should suffice.

Doors and windows will be added with the right shade of brown or black tones, but without being painted too dark or giving the effect of black holes. Remember that here too there will be fine details added (door latches, window frames, etc.).

c. After the layout has dried well, it is time to work out the picture, which demands concentration and endurance. First draw the most important lines finely (gutters, gables, chimneys, etc.). Select a neutral gray tone for this; it can be broken with a bit of blue or chestnut. Roof tiles and the structures of balconies or wooden coverings should also be drawn now. Use a fine brush, so you can paint all the details clearly, and the same naturally applies to the surroundings of the house, in which branches and larger groups of leaves can now be painted. Be sure to make the growing things true to life, so that the observer will recognize the type and location of the tree or shrub. Shadows and particular depths of the motif can also be stressed by being formed exactly like the model.

65 For a picture of several buildings, an old-town scene with its nooks and crannies is especially charming.

d. After the paint has dried well once again, the last task follows, with all the fine details being worked out. This includes the smallest items, such as house lights or even lightning rods. Add in all these details in the appropriate colors, and give the trees and shrubs their final appearance as well. The white with which the light reflections can be achieved (for example, on window glass, water surfaces or even plants) does its work well here.

At the very end, we paint the bright spots of color of flowers and the glowing elements, such as those of shutters and awnings.

66 A landscape painting, shown in three steps (exact description in text).

a

b

c

67 An old half-timbered house as an example of building painting. Such motifs are especially suitable for wall plates or porcelain platters.

Christmas Plates (New Year Plates)

The so-called New Year plates, now as before, enjoy great popularity in many families, and some of them have become desirable collectors' items. For many it is fascinating to acquire an unbroken series. The motifs are very different and not to be found on plates alone (Christmas bells or various tree decorations are also possible).

The choice of motifs offers you a multitude of possibilities, from fairy-tale scenes to landscapes and wintery pictures. But wall plates in modern styles are also possible. Begin by choosing a motif that suits your taste, and determine the colors to be used. New Year plates are generally done in a single color and brightened up only with a few gold or platinum effects. For a long time, cobalt or royal blue has been popular. It forms an ideal contrast to the white of the porcelain as a component of snowy and other winter motifs.

I would recommend, especially if you wish to institute an ongoing series, that you concentrate on a very definite theme (for example, childhood scenes, landscapes, nativity scenes, etc.). Thus you will appeal to the collector who will want to acquire the new piece every year.

In general, the work process is as already described in the *Landscape Painting* section. The techniques and steps are much the same.

a. First draw the chosen motif precisely. If that appears to be too difficult for this motif, then prepare a stencil and draw it with charcoal.

b. Draw in the most important contours with dark cobalt blue. Put in the first deeply shadowed areas on the roofs and gables. Trees or bushes can also be indicated lightly now. Bright sky and landscape areas can be applied with a wide brush and allowed to dry well. To apply "soft" surfaces, use a stipple brush in order to make the transitions smooth and quiet. Let the entire layout dry well!

c. Now we can begin to work out the details. This is likewise done in the same manner as in landscape painting. If you are using just one color, it is best to divide the tone values into three levels. Paint dark, medium, and light tones.

d. In the process, all the details are copied exactly from the model or the pattern. Use a fine brush of medium strength.

In case you are working with glazing cobalt blue, here are a few tips: Quietly apply the darkest tones to the piece very thickly and almost pastelike. This paint is a so-called sinking-in paint, which means that it penetrates slightly into the glaze during firing (there are, to be sure, other blue shades that are also suitable and do not need to be burned so hot). This sinking-in blue must be burned at about 1100° C in order to bring out the soft impression that so many collectors treasure in New Year plates. So before you begin your work, make sure that your firing apparatus can reach such high temperatures.

e. When you add the numerals of the year, make sure that they fit into the picture and are not too separate and isolated. There are many ways that this can be done. One can paint them on a building, present them as numerals, or scratch them into the snow, as in our example.

f. When firing, you must, as noted, pay attention to the type of paint and its melting point. We have deliberately not yet added any precious-metal paint, since this would burn up at a melting temperature of over 1000° C.

g. After the object has cooled, gold or platinum can be added to the painting. With cobalt blue painting, use it extremely sparingly, so as not to push the beautiful blue into the background. In most cases, it is used only for small stars or decorations on Christmas trees or houses anyway. There should be a balance of brilliance between the blue and the gold. I would also like to recommend to you an enclosing ring around the entire motif if you are painting a wall plate.

68 Varying decor for a porcelain bell to hang on a Christmas tree.

Children's Motifs

Youthful motifs for small children's utensils are an extremely popular type of decoration. Many such pieces keep children company over many years. Of course such things can be had in the trade, but it is something different when Mom or Dad has personally conjured up something for their offspring. Such motifs have a particular charm when they are based on pictures from children's books. But self-designed figures too, such as the clown in Illustration 73, quickly bring cheer to a child's heart. You should undertake a search for subject matter in a completely child-like manner, ingenuous and naive. There will be so many possibilities that making a choice will often be difficult. Animals, toys and fairy-tale figures are just as possible as imaginary creatures or even simple symbols. You may also want to follow the inclinations of your youngsters and choose a favorite sport, a beloved teddy bear, etc.

In terms of composition, you can proceed unconventionally. Avoid an overly stiff arrangement and overly pale colors. Children like bright, glaring things best. Keep in mind too that small children in particular like to "discover" something on the plate, and that eating should be a pleasure for them. When the food conceals something, it will be eaten up twice as willingly if there is a surprise waiting under it.

Once again, you can make the drawing freehand or with a stencil. The stencil is particularly to be recommended when you use motifs from children's literature, so as to make the painting as much like the original as possible. It is best to begin by outlining the figures or objects in the appropriate color with brush or pen and then, after letting the outlines dry well, painting in the surfaces.

Finally, colorful borders on plates and cups are very appropriate for children's porcelain. The technical process used in this step can be taken from the material on gold decoration.

69-70 A small pitcher and a bowl with childhood motifs.

71 A New Year plate in cobalt blue, with gold elements.

72 Simple childhood motifs on a cocoa mug and a plate.

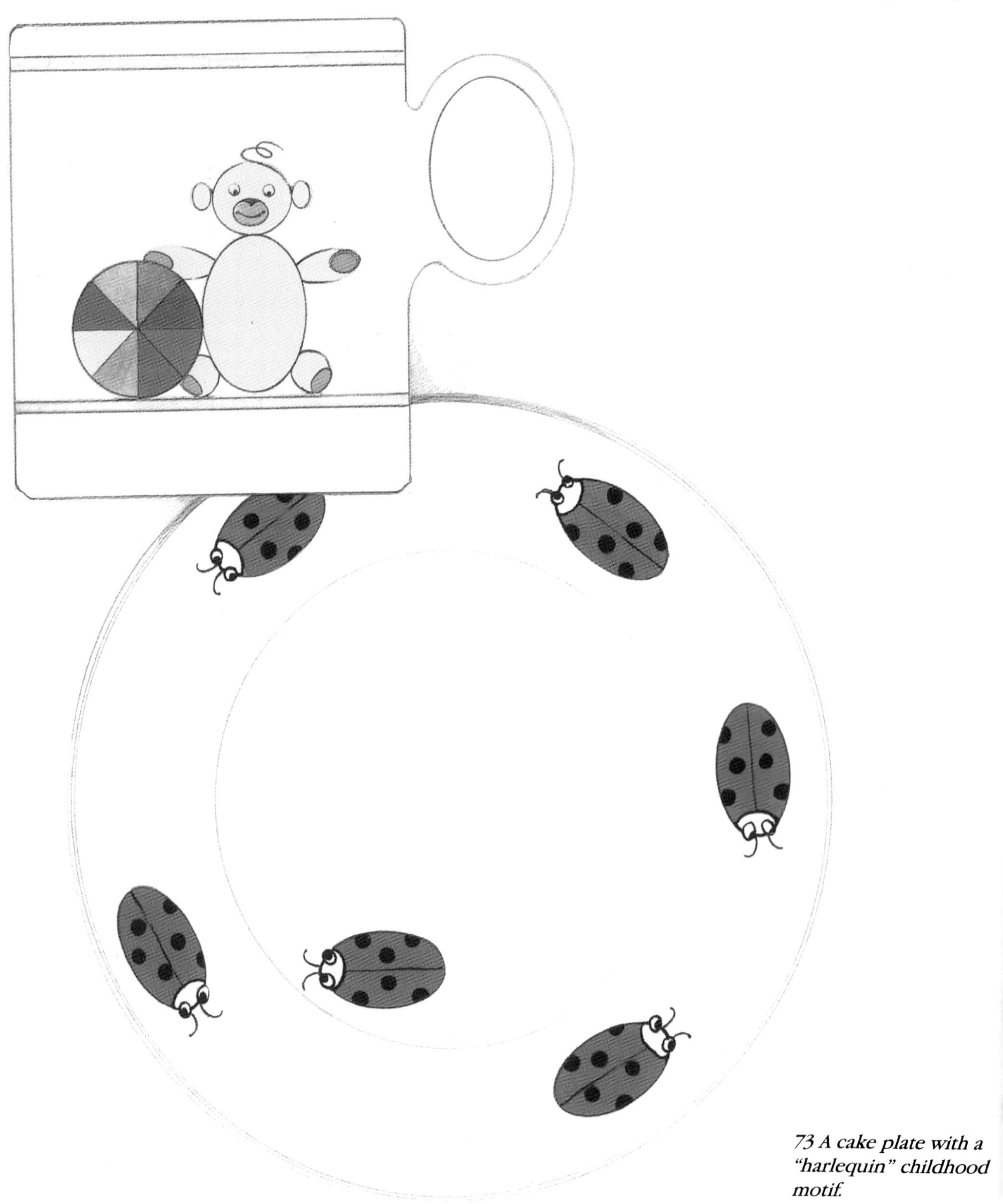

73 A cake plate with a "harlequin" childhood motif.

74 A tulip painted in copperplate technique:
a. Layout
b. Finished

75 A small flower bouquet in the typical stroke technique of copperplate painting.

Copperplate Painting

Copperplate painting is certainly the most laborious technique of porcelain painting, and it also has a great European tradition. The flower painters in Meissen based their work on copperplates and woodcuts and used them as models. Around 1720 this was the most widespread technique of portraying nature. It was thus quite natural for these studies to be utilized in decorating the only recently discovered "white gold." In thousands of variations, these first steps on the way to modern-day flower painting have become known all over the world. For the porcelain fan, it is most interesting to study all of these individual examples and use them for his own training. It is not easy, and I would really advise only the experienced painter to attempt this technique. There is no lack of models at hand. One need only think of the great treasure that Maria Sybilla Merian (1647-1717) created, thousands of nature studies from all over the world. And she did not limit herself to the study of flowers either, but also included fruits and insects in all their delicacy and accuracy of detail.

The charm of copperplate painting is surely its uniqueness, namely that of putting the entire motif together out of many, many individual strokes. Thus no complete shadowed areas are formed; rather every little bit of darkness is stroked into existence. Here too, it is naturally a question of putting the shadows in the right places. The layout on the porcelain is done in very tender color tones, followed by the working out on the porcelain in very gentle strokes. The old masters did not always think of the direction of growth here, and at times their painting seems a bit folded and dried-out. Thus it has been called "tried flower painting." In the further development of this painting technique, the change was made at various factories to making the strokes run in the direction of growth, which gives the flowers somewhat more liveliness.

When this gentle layout has dried well, we can begin to work out the picture. The basic requirement for this is naturally an excellent brush, which, as already described, one should cut out first. Here in particular, an ugly unwanted stroke of the brush makes itself noticed in a very negative way.

This technique is often somewhat too difficult for the beginner and does not lead to the hoped-for success. Therefore you should first try various motifs on paper and get acquainted with the unique technique.

The paints also demand a very particular treatment, and it takes some practice to keep them in hand. Let us take the copper green as a color of its own. This special color has the unique quality of becoming transparent only after firing. That means it is first underlaid in black, and then one puts the copper green over it in two layers. The black drawing at first disappears completely under the green. While firing, the green becomes transparent and the drawing becomes visible again. This color, though, is used exclusively for plant green. Since it requires a certain routine, it should also remain reserved for the experienced painter (Ill. 75).

The other colors are somewhat like those of manneristic painting in treatment and application, except that one should dilute them somewhat, so that they do not have too glaring and poisonous an appearance. The originals of copperplates, in fact, exist only in very moderate tones, and really loud colors are the exceptions. There are also several other rules to keep in mind while working out the picture. For example, the yellow should not be worked out with gray, but this task should be done with a dark brown tone. The precise composition of this painting technique can be studied in many works in one of countless art books.

FANTASY DESIGNS

Every porcelain painter would like to produce a motif designed by himself instead of just utilizing types of decor taken from the classics. Every individual should naturally develop his own ideas, so as to find his own style. Here one can only give some encouragement and discuss the technical processes. If these designs are to be up-to-date in terms of style, you will orient yourself to present-day trends or to specific fashion colors anyway. Note Illustration 77.

a. Begin by using the crayon to draw in the contours of the painting lightly. It is important for the drawing to have a balanced composition of the chosen decor. Thus you should not just concentrate on one side of the plate surface, but on an even division of the individual segments.

In our example, there are mosaic-like fields which constantly vary in size and shape. I have made them to interlock like a jigsaw puzzle, so as to achieve a unity of the picture.

b. Now comes the painting in color. In a soft violet, we lay out the individual fields evenly. Rub the paint on somewhat oilier (thick oil), to make the paint spread evenly. When all the segments are painted in, put the object or objects into the stovepipe for a few minutes so it will dry well.

c. In the third step, we give the individual sections some structure, which livens up the entire motif and gives it an almost crystalline effect. For this, use a dark violet, to which some blue can be added for additional brilliance of color.

The individual working-out lines can be set in the individual surfaces in star shape. With somewhat smaller individual segments, a nicely stroked line will suffice, or even a small lines on the edge of the area. Always add the lines from inside outward (and let the paint dry well again after this painting procedure).

d. The completion of this imaginative decor shall now form a border made in platinum, which is applied with a fine brush. First draw in the spaces between the violet fields gently and carefully. Prevent the color and platinum from overlapping each other, if possible. If it should happen anyway that the two overlap and are fired that way, that is no reason to worry. In these places there will generally appear a tiny dark border, which will scarcely disturb the motif as a whole, and can sometimes be quite charming.

A few individually distributed spots of platinum around the individual surfaces give the painting additional charm.

Finally, form the border with thin lines of platinum around the edges. Make one border completely on the outside and one on the inside of the rim area. The exact directions for this are found in the *Gold Decoration* chapter.

76 Free flower and border decor on a plate.

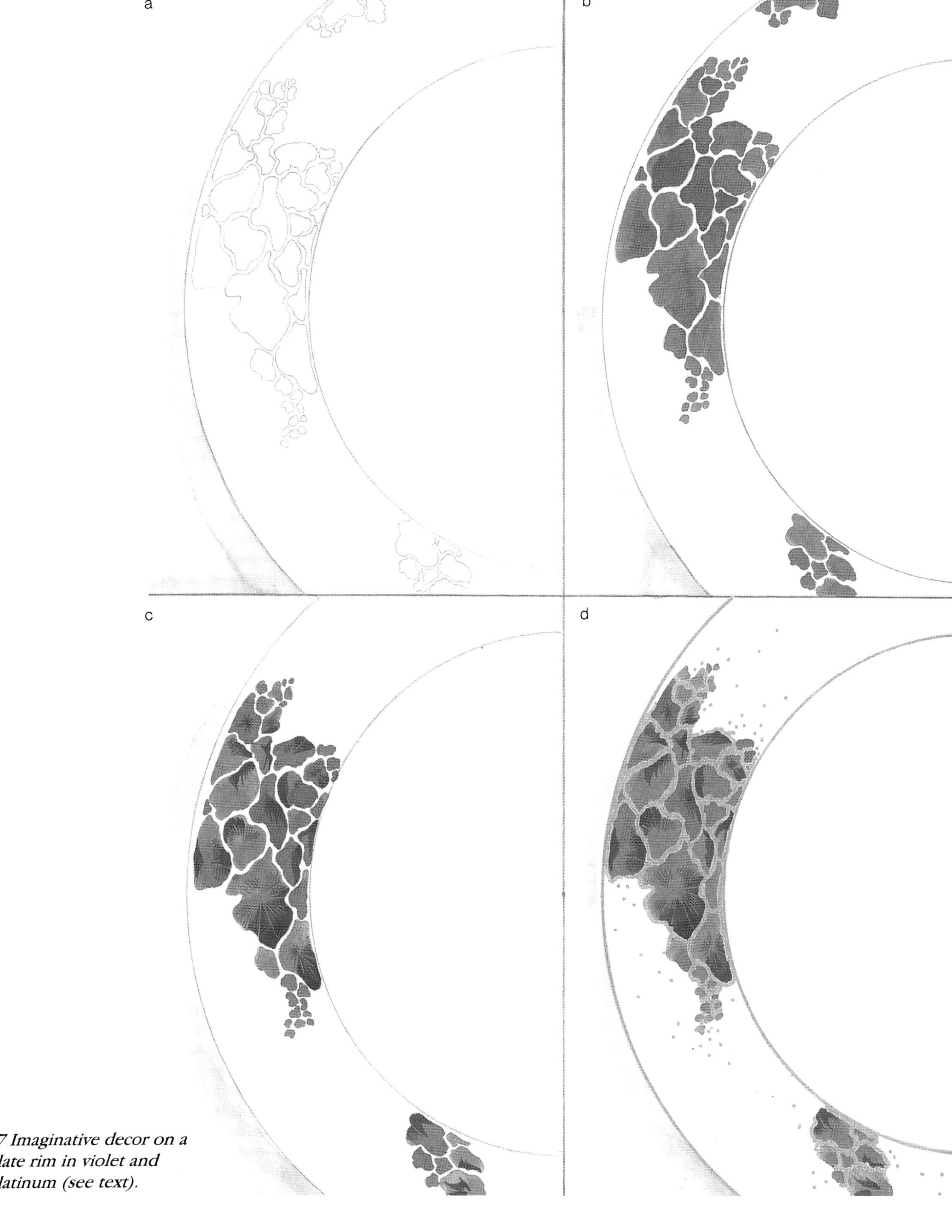

77 Imaginative decor on a plate rim in violet and platinum (see text).

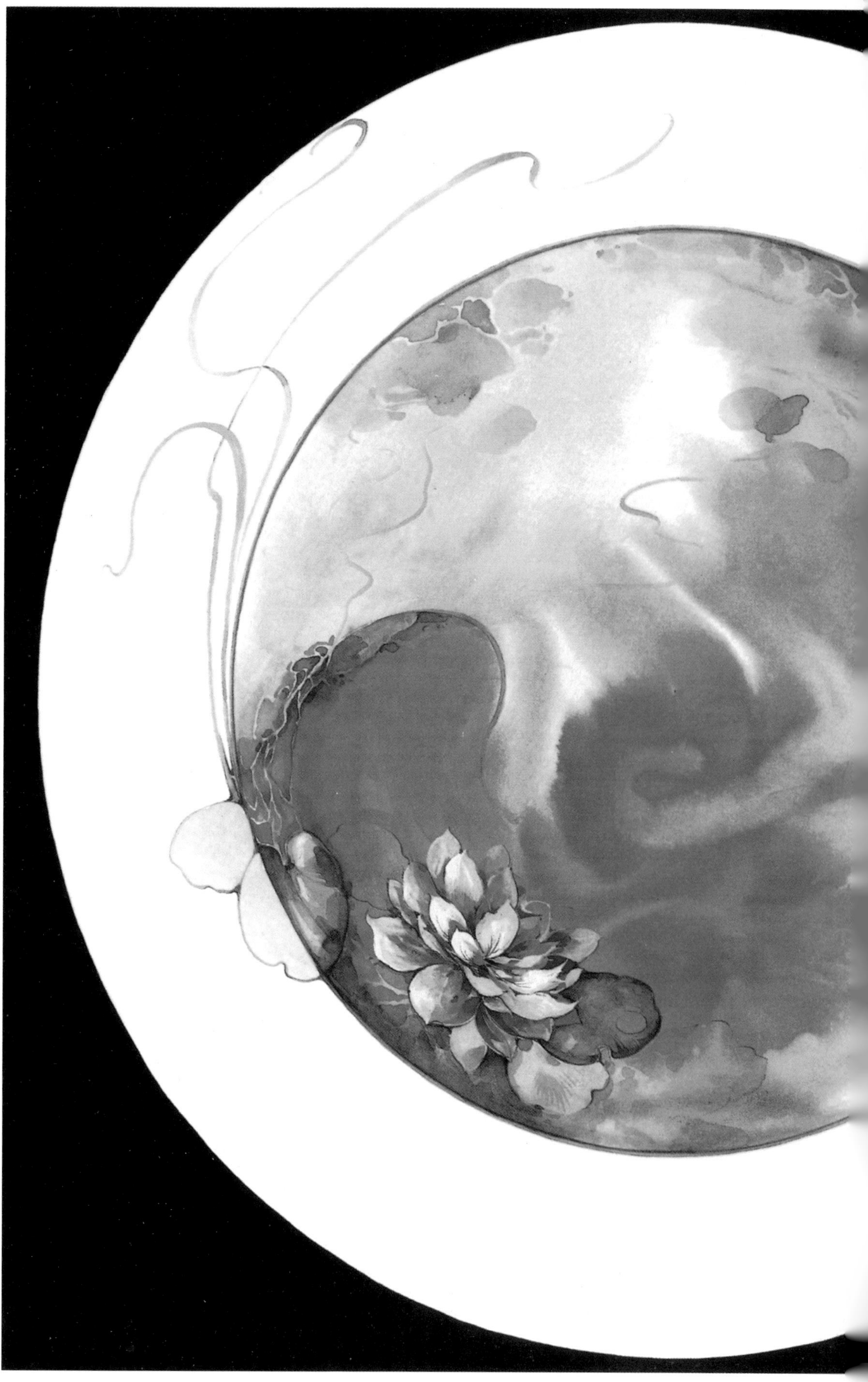

78 Imaginative decor for a plate center with gentle transitions to the rim of the plate (waterlily motif).

79 Freely developed "Red Horse" decor for flat areas. Naturally, the colors can be switched at will here.

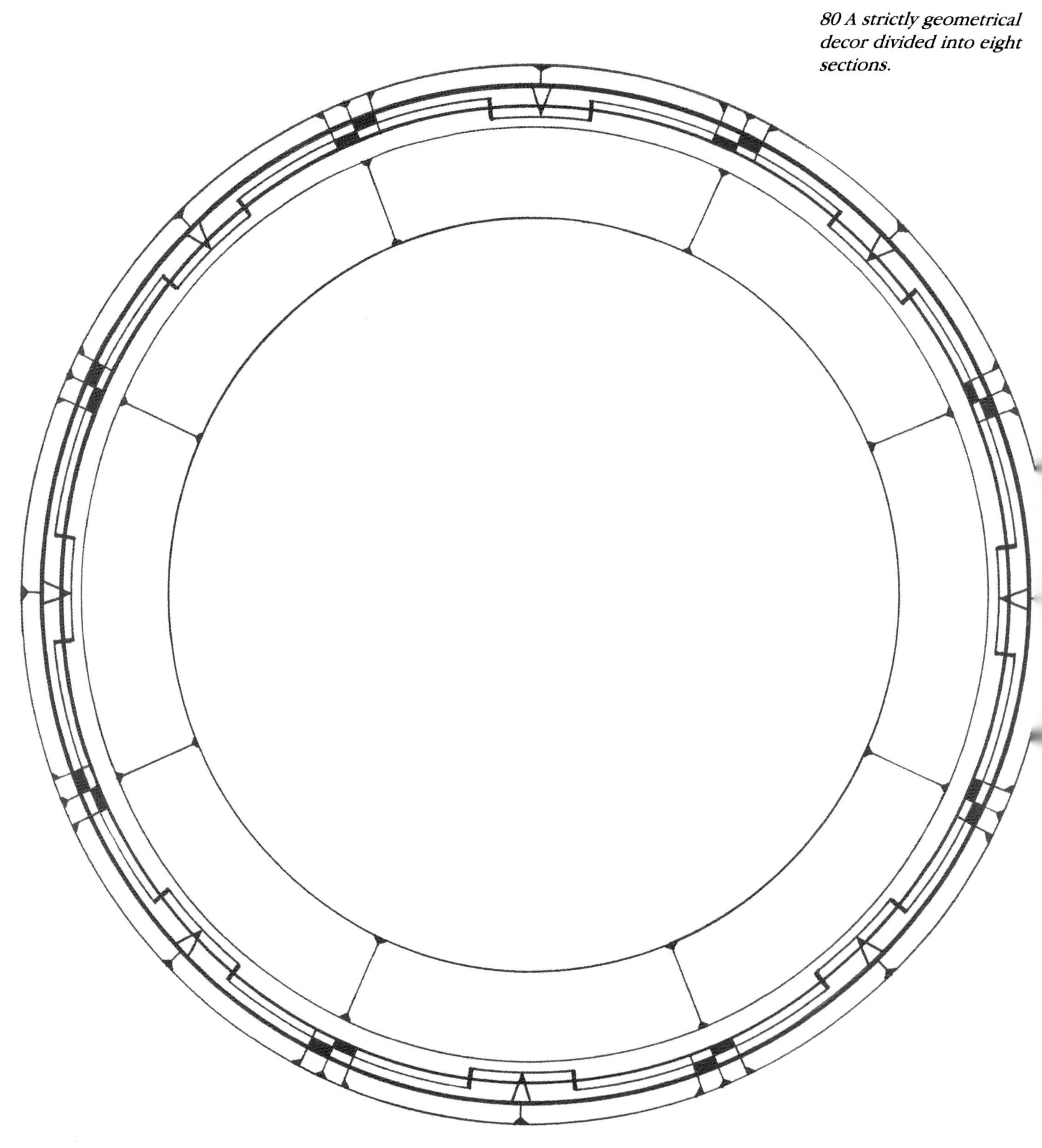

80 A strictly geometrical decor divided into eight sections.

Decorative Motifs

Decorative motifs actually include all imaginable types of decoration. To be sure, we find, as the name implies, many details in them that are also utilized in other decorations. The individual elements extend from colorful bands with bows to simple borders to opulent edge motifs. You can get ideas for them anywhere, just by looking, for example, at how jewelers form their work and using impressions gained from the world of nature. In the process, a broad spectrum opens to you. Even though there are many classic patterns, personally developed ideas are no less charming. Their arrangement on the piece itself should be determined by the shape of it. Often they can be worked on varying surface reliefs. Neutral shapes without raised areas in the white surfaces naturally can be painted most easily, since the course of a decorative stripe, for instance, can run absolutely free, without having to follow a design. For the most part, such a decorative stripe is laid out along the flat surfaces on the rim. This leaves the middle of the plate free and lets the food create its own effect.

On the hollow pieces, the arrangement, as already noted, can be formed completely freely. Often it can be noted—and also suits the "porcelain taste" of many collectors—that bows and ribbons swing lightly into the flat surfaces and can be formed interestingly with knots and loops. In addition, flowers, branches or soft lines can liven up the effect. The colors should be chosen according to the selected model.

—First draw the motif schematically with the crayon (if you have a very detailed pattern, you can also prepare a stencil and fit it to the piece).

—Now a contouring of the motif similar to that of Indian painting is recommended (with pen or brush, according to the color situation). Ribbons or flowers can also be laid on. Again, make sure that special reliefs and decorations harmonize with the style.

—Finally, after a good drying, the fine working-out can be done, with the precious metal details added at the very end.

Ornaments

Ornamentation for the decoration of porcelain objects has a tradition that reaches back to the beginning of human history. Mankind began early to decorate objects in daily use, such as pitchers and drinking cups, and provide them with ornamental elements. The patterns for this were taken from nature, and the structure of a leaf, a shadow that happened by chance, or the shape of a cloud always gave man's imagination new inspiration. Most ornaments also show a certain regularity or symmetry: On a plate, for example, the ornamental segments usually lie beside or near each other in the same form.

For special use in porcelain painting, though, one can limit oneself to a simple basic design. We generally differentiate the four-, six-, and—the maximum for beginners—eight-part divisions. The chosen division naturally determines how often a decorative motif appears.

For decorative elements in particular, there are possible choices in every imaginable cultural epoch. And naturally it must also be remembered that the decorative part has to suit the shape of the object. But this does not mean that the porcelain to be painted always has to be in the style of the chosen decor. Almost all timeless, flat pieces, without any flourishes or reliefs, are better suited to ornamental rim decoration, since one can apply the painted border more easily and without pressure from existing designs.

Inspiration for decor does not need to come solely from older porcelain objects themselves; it can also be found in particular in the literature of architecture, painting and fashion history, and the stucco techniques such as intarsia, in great richness.

81 A goblet vase with decorative band of flower segments (see details in 81a).

81a ▷

Just a few tips now as to the work processes (using a plate as an example): Divide the rim of a plate into the desired number of segments (four, six or eight). To do this, we use the already mentioned crayon, with which we can also mark out a series of additional points of orientation. First, though, the precise center of the object has to be located, which often is made easier because, as a result of manufacturing methods, there is a small raised spot in the center of the plate. This point, which serves as a point of orientation, can be seen by holding the plate up to the light at an angle. If this little hill is unseen or seen very faintly, the midpoint can be determined with a ruler. Set the zero marking of the ruler at any place on the rim of the plate and slowly move the ruler back and forth until you have determined the greatest diameter of the plate. This can then be marked with the crayon and the halfway point can be marked with a dot. From this central point one need only mark a line at a 90-degree angle to divide the plate perfectly into four parts. The four sections can be divided further with a protractor to form eight divisions. For uneven divisions, one can avoid otherwise necessary procedures by using the so-called dividing screen. It is a practical tool to use in forming certain flat areas, and Illustration 82 shows exactly how to use it. Thin cardboard is a sufficiently flexible and sturdy material of which to make it.

In the radiating star that has resulted from drawing the dividing lines, the individual planned details can now be added. You can easily use patterns or ornamenting rulers when the motif allows. If you still need borders or fine lines in the pattern, use the border screen (see *Gold Decoration*) and a fine thin brush. These lines, moreover, should be applied right after dividing the segments, since they allow a good orientation and give the whole pattern a certain "frame." It is particularly recommended that all ornamental details be laid out first in the appropriate color and then colored, as is described in the *Indian Painting* section. Whether you use a brush or a pen for the outlines is up to you and the design plans. Naturally, stencils are also possible for larger details; Illustrations 95-96 show the precise work processes.

82 A disc used to divide flat surfaces into equal parts:
Thirds
Quarters
Sixths
Eighths

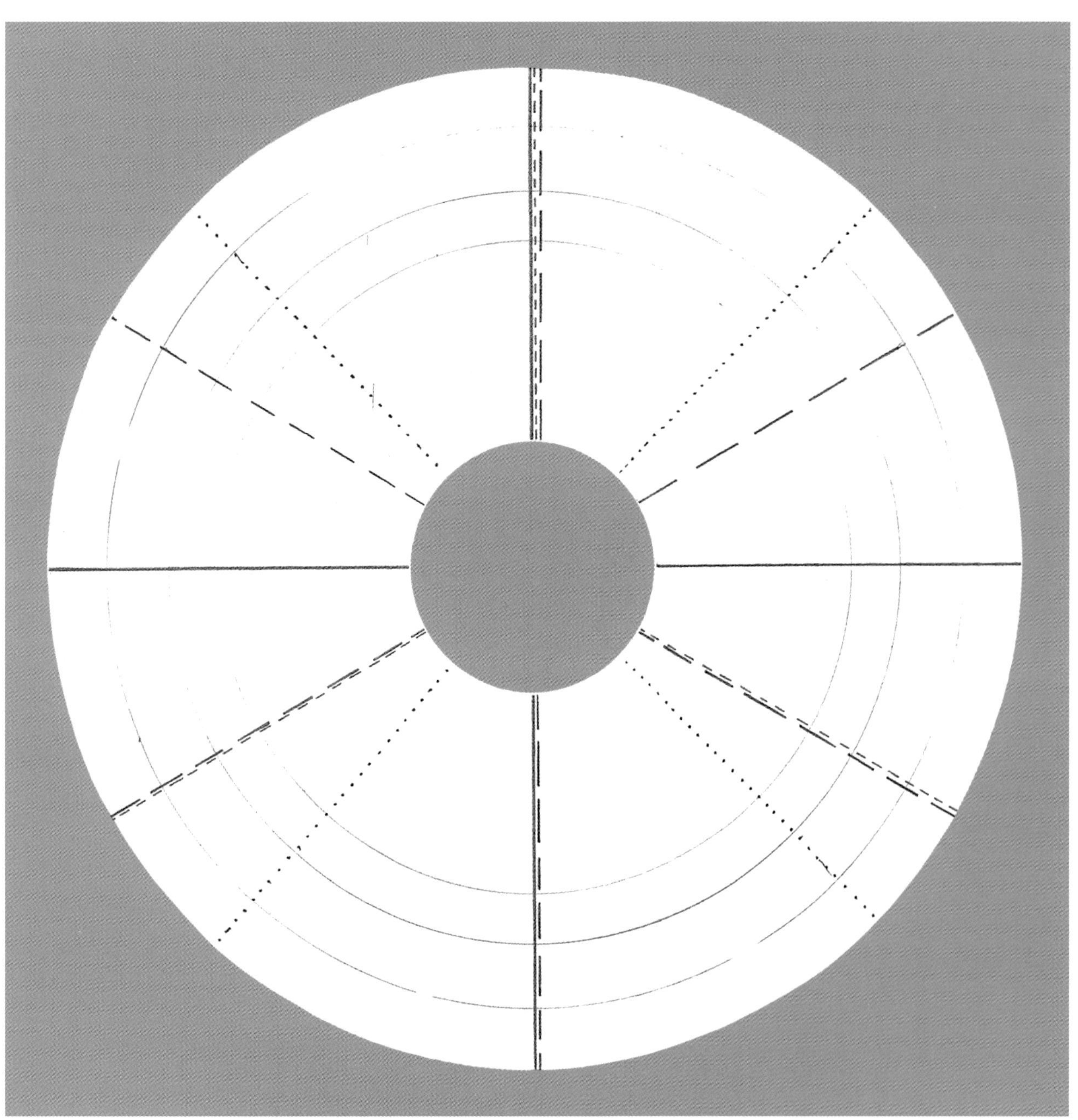

83-84 Two examples of simple geometrical ornaments that can be extended for borders and continuing decors.

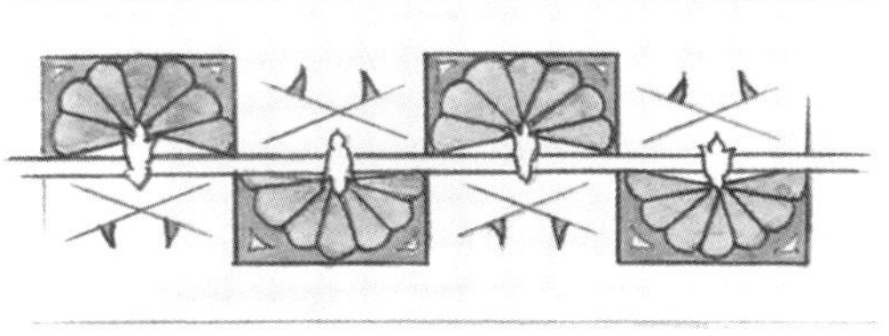

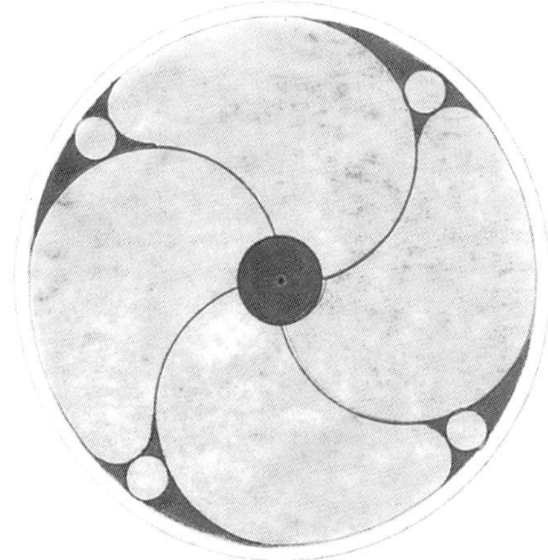

85 Simple ribbon decor in three colors. The simple pattern lets the decorations create a young, free effect.

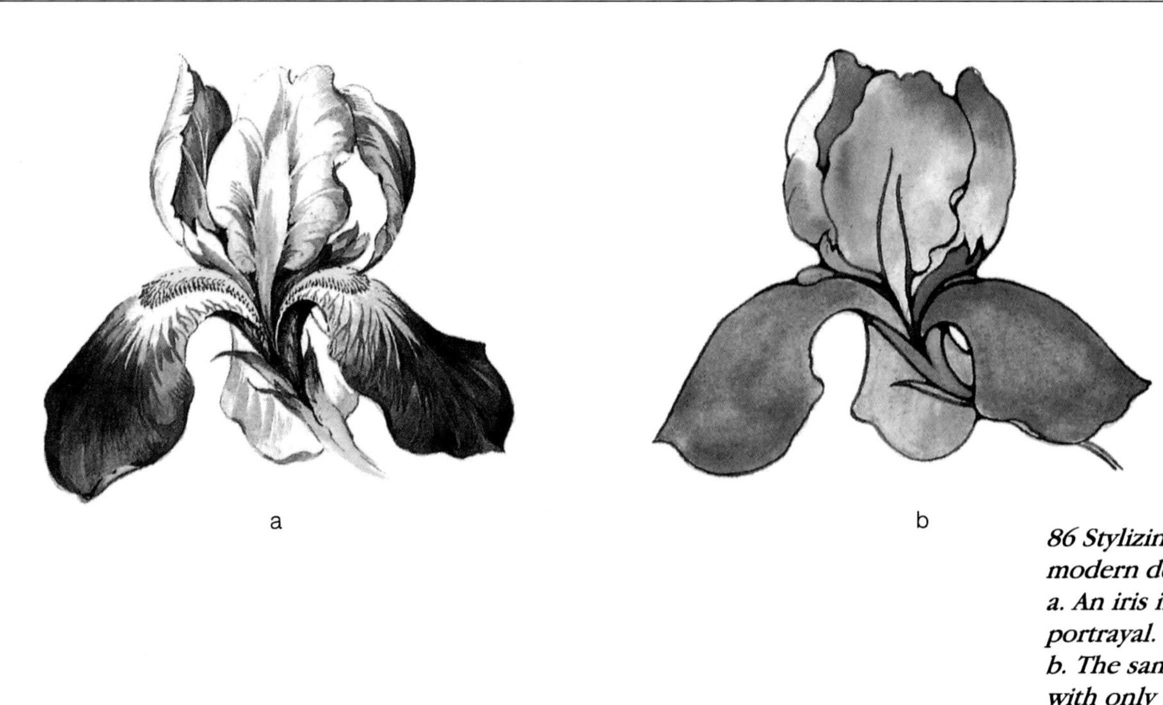

a

b

86 Stylizing a flower for modern decor:
a. An iris in naturalistic portrayal.
b. The same flower stylized, with only the essential contours retained.
c. The stylized iris included in a colored rim.

c

87 Orchids, with their filigree structure, are especially suitable for stylized portrayals.

Stylized Flowers

The stylizing of flowers has become important, since in more and more factories they have gone over to working with decals, and also as, for reasons of their clients' preferences and various fashion trends and epochs of style, the decoration of porcelain began to change. The greatest "blossoming" of the partially abstract-looking flowers can probably be ascribed to the era of Art Nouveau. In unbelievable variety, magical paintings were developed, some of them using completely new techniques, most of which have been completely forgotten by now.

Here, though, we want to limit ourselves to reliable hand-painting. First take a flower of your choice and, using nature studies, try to seize upon its essential characteristics (shapes, signs of growth, colors, particulars). Illustration 86 shows this process, using the iris as an example.

a. Here we see the flower in its naturalistic appearance, with all the details, stamens, petals, ribs, color tones—everything is portrayed as it naturally appears.

b. Here we limit ourselves to the outer contours and the most essential central ribs of the individual petals; details like stamens and small markings are eliminated. In terms of color, we can now move into the world of fantasy; you can portray the flowers completely according to your own taste.

c. The stylized iris is now part of a colored plate rim. The main color of the flower should harmonize with the color of the rim, and of course color combinations are also possible, but always make sure that the various shades can go together. You will find a tremendous amount of examples in the copious literature of Art Nouveau.

For decorating, try to select porcelains that have no relief patterns, and in which the decor provides the primary effect.

Edge Decorations

Edge decorations are also very much in demand because there are many porcelain fans who want the food on the plate to "have an effect" and do not want the plate to be dominated by the decor. Here the painting merely provides a frame surrounding the food. As a result, edge decorations are usually made unobtrusive. They amount to relatively simple plate-rim decor that is effective by its very simplicity (Ill. 91).

a. Create the motif according to your own designs or from patterns. For optimal utilization of the rim, use the rim screen as described under *Gold Decoration*.

In our example, the rim is cobalt blue with purple flowers set into it. Naturally, other color combinations are also possible.

b. Begin by laying on the outer edge evenly. To do this, use the rim screen to achieve a constant, even line all around. The brush size should be selected according to the width of the line to be painted. By the way, here it is not necessarily required that the paint be completely smooth and even, since a little unevenness makes the ring fresh and lively. Now set out the white surfaces for the flower petals, since the green must be added in during the next work process. For small petal shapes, the palette knife is sufficient. With a properly small brush, draw the thin lines toward the interior of the plate.

c. The next step is to paint the tender green and purple tones of the flowers. Let them dry well!

Now paint in the finer details such as petal ribs and flower structures in the colored elements. For the green leaves, I recommend a light brown, and for the purple blossoms a dark carmine red.

d. To finish the decoration, add white spots to the cobalt-blue rim and contrasting blue ones on the white surfaces.

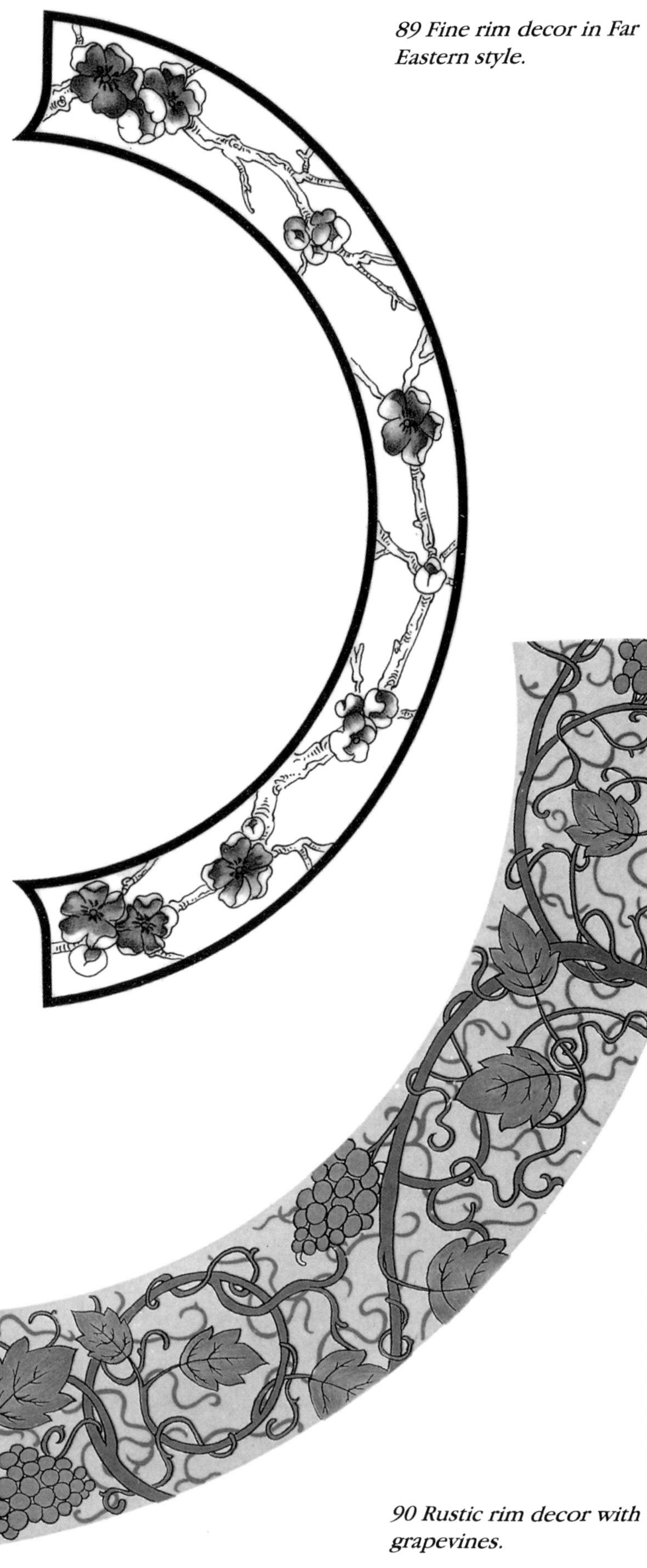

89 Fine rim decor in Far Eastern style.

90 Rustic rim decor with grapevines.

91 Cobalt blue rim decor with flowers added (see p. 88).

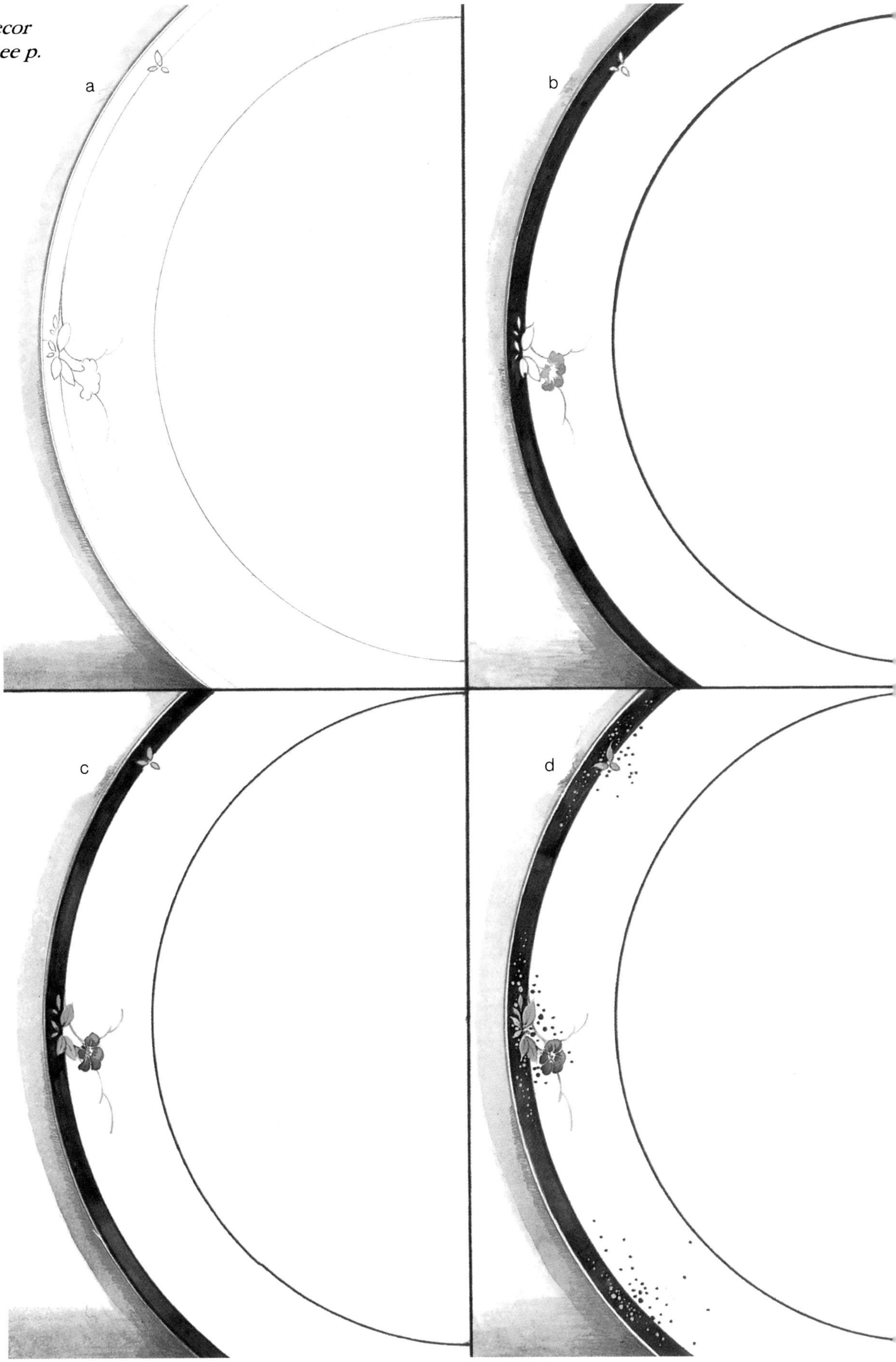

a

b

c

d

92 A decorative motif of bright-colored flowers held by blue ribbons.

93 A teapot with a decorative stripe and forget-me-nots.

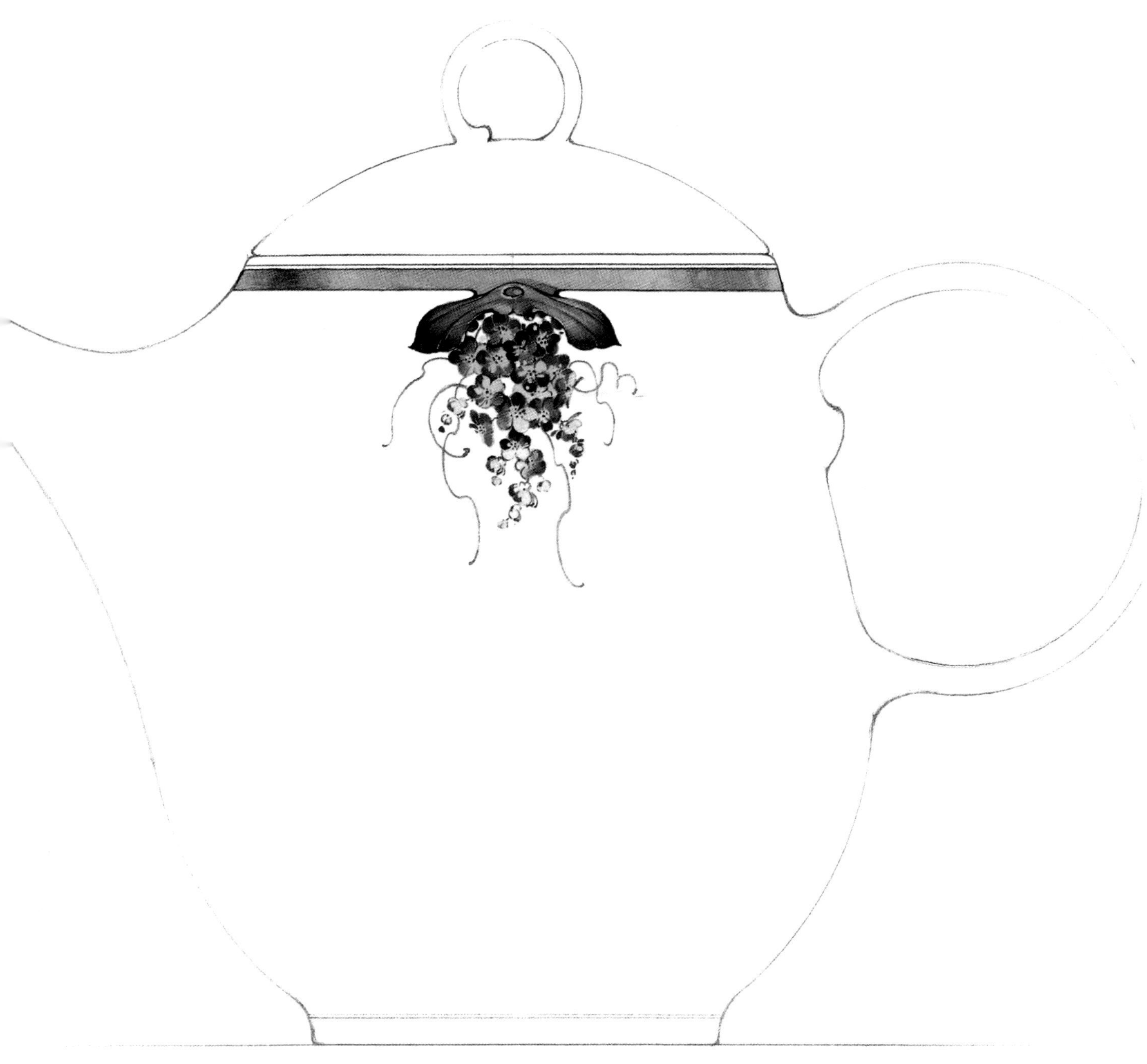

94 A Chinese pheasant motif in richly colored form (directions in text).

INDIAN AND FAR EASTERN PAINTING

The so-called Indian painting on porcelain has a strikingly graphic character, as opposed to the purely painting techniques already discussed. These colorful patterns with their almost ornamental-looking nature have their origin in the porcelain factories of the Far East. Long before Böttger invented European porcelain, merchants and dealers brought these works of art to Europe, and at numerous royal courts there was already a desire to prepare these paintings themselves and thus save on the high expenses, as well as to possess the mysterious monopoly on this "white gold." When porcelain was then produced in Europe, naturally the motifs used in distant China were utilized, adopting the figures in scarcely changed form. Only gradually was there a trend toward making their own designs. But the basic type remained the same: stylized portrayals based on religion, nature, hunting, fables, and everyday life.

We would like to begin by limiting ourselves to the ground rules of this specialized painting, so as to learn the painting techniques and processes of Far Eastern decor. Ideas and motifs can be found in a series of lacquer paintings, India ink drawings, and woodcuts by many masters from China, Japan, and also Korea. Of course the motifs used in them always have their own traditions and links with the religion of their country, and our imitations, whether samurai scenes or legendary Ming dragons, will always lack something. But this very variety can be utilized in our porcelain painting.

Equipment

The equipment is more or less the same as that used in the painting techniques already covered. We need only examine the drawing pen and the stencil more precisely. Since this is a very graphic manner of painting, the pen naturally takes on a great importance. All the other painting tools known to us—brush, spatula, palette knife, etc.—are also used here. The only new addition is the stencil cloth, with which we apply the crude outlines of the motif through the stencil. More of that in the next section. As for brushes, we need various sizes, to be able to color different-sized surfaces. As before, keep an assortment of different sizes and thicknesses of brush hairs on hand. We must be able to paint very finely as well as create large spots with consistent color strength. Since the brushes are used only to paint in the previously marked contours, the bodies of the brushes must be relatively strong, and their points do not play an essential role. Brushes that are already "painted out" and no longer have very good points are suitable for this work. For fine details of the motifs, on the other hand, a brush with a good point and a medium body is suitable.

A small steel pen about 2.5 cm long, such as are readily available in the trade, makes a suitable drawing pen. With proper maintenance and care, such a pen will fulfill its tasks for many months. If the pen should show a somewhat rough, scratchy point when first used, careful smoothing on a very fine whetstone, with water, will help. The smooth surface for painting that the porcelain glaze presents makes this necessary, since the desired line would otherwise be broken, and the paint cannot be applied with the desired smoothness.

The stencil cloth is actually a small stencil bag and serves to apply the stencil charcoal to the stencil. It should consist of a dust-free piece of cloth which one fills with a soft material (wadding or the like) and ties with string at the upper end, which is drawn together (Ill. 95c).

The last new tool that we need to mention is the needle for use in making the stencil itself. It consists of a pointed needle that is set into a handle of wood (Ill. 95b). This instrument can be made easily by the painter.

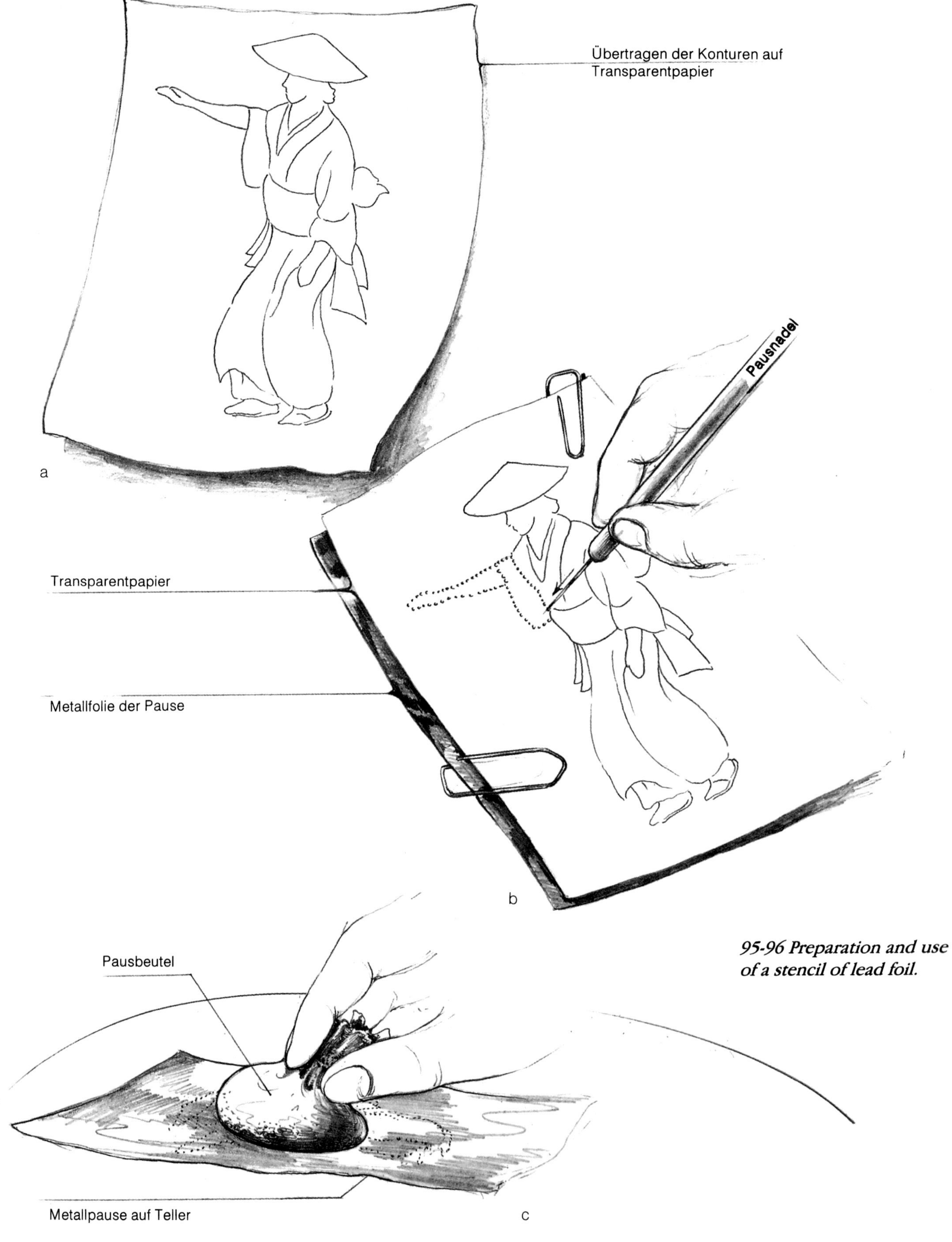

95-96 Preparation and use of a stencil of lead foil.

a

b

96 ▷

c

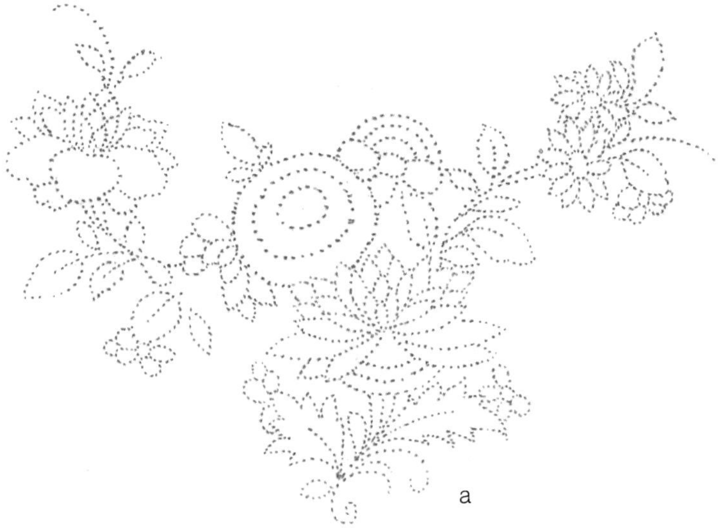

a

b

97 Stylized flowers in Indian painting style, showing three steps (exact description in text).

The Stencil

The stencil is used primarily to transfer motifs which must look as alike as possible on several pieces. By using it, one saves oneself laborious drawing of a design that is constantly the same. Nevertheless every piece is different, for no 100% identical copy is ever made, for only the basic outline of the picture is transferred to every piece of the service. Every piece also bears the individual signature of the artist, so that there will never be two fully identical pieces.

The stencil itself can be prepared quickly. Here too, follow the progression that is shown in Illustrations 95-96.

a. Select the motif and determine the most important contours. One need not limit oneself to graphic painting. Landscapes and such can also be applied with stencils, which is advisable when they are to be painted on several pieces in the same size and shape.

One begins by taking a piece of transparent paper and tracing the most important lines and outlines of the desired picture on it (Ill. 95a).

b. This piece of paper is then laid over the actual stencil, which should be made of a strong metal foil, and fastened in place with paper clips. Lead foil is most suitable, since this can easily be fitted to the curved parts of the white dish later on. But a strong aluminum foil is also usable, though it will not last as long.

Now we take the stencil needle and make small holes along the lines, so that later the stencil charcoal will pass through them to sketch the contours (Ill. 95b). When we have punctured all the lines of the decor motif, we removed the transparent paper and have a finished stencil (Ill. 96a). Check it by looking through the holes of the stencil toward a source of light, to make sure the work has been done properly. The second stencil, which we have now produced in the transparent paper, is, moreover, well suited to work on wood or paper.

c. Now we need only place the lead foil on the desired object and we can begin to stencil. This is done with the help of the charcoal bag—in which we place a little stencil charcoal, which we have obtained from fine drawing charcoal (by rubbing it with fine sandpaper)—which we move lightly along the lines (Ill. 95c). The fine bits of charcoal which now pass through the holes form our outline for the pen drawing (Ill. 96b).

As for preserving the stencils, it can be said that with proper treatment—it is best to put each one alone in a small box—they can be used for a long time without being damaged. If they happen to get bent, though, they can be fitted again easily. Tearing, though, is almost always the end for a stencil, since the pattern often becomes damaged.

Drawing With The Pen

Making pen drawings on porcelain takes some practice, since the paint, taken from the spatula, must run freely out of the pen without spreading too far. A clear stripe in strong color is required. This is the basic difficulty of this type of painting. The color must therefore be prepared exactly right so that it is easily paintable and yet not too thin and runny. You should make the paint mix very tin (with turpentine). Add a few drops of thick oil and just a very little bit of oil of cloves. Oil of cloves keeps the paint fresh and usable for a long time, but it has a very "spreading" effect. Thus use these three oils for the first mixing of the pigment powder. If the mixed paint should begin to dry while in use, add a little more turpentine to it.

One should not forget that the drawn lines come into contact with oil again, namely when the drawn surfaces are painted in color. The lines can dissolve easily then and spoil the pattern. An intermediate firing is recommended to the beginner, so as to be sure the drawing is secure, after which he can finish the painting in peace. Pen drawing is not a technique that cannot be learned, quite the opposite, and it is an extremely charming technique that can also be used for a number of other types of painting.

You can also try mixing the colors for the drawing with a sugar solution and painting with them, since this will avoid a reaction between the two paints (water/oil) when you finish the painting with oil later.

Stylized Flowers and Birds

To begin with, here are a few rules that should be followed in Indian painting:

—Clean the piece and check it for any flaws that can be found.

—Stencil the motif and then draw with the pen in the desired color, then let dry.

—Put on the lines if the motif requires it, then let them dry.

—Paint the contours in the proper color. Make sure to get the right color strength and make the mix correspond to the original.

—Add the gold elements that are not directly on the colors.

—Do the first firing at the highest possible temperature for the paint.

—Now gold elements that go directly onto already painted and burned areas can be painted into the pattern. Powdered gold is best suited to this, since it flows freely and thus does not sink into the paint.

—Do the second firing at a lower temperature (400-500° C should be enough).

—Polish the gold.

The Chinese motifs made their way along trade routes to Europe via India. This gave them the incorrect name of Indian painting. From then on, the majority of all East Asiatic styles bore this name, although they often originated elsewhere. The name prevails to this day, and so we too shall go on speaking of Indian painting when it includes Asiatic patterns.

Many of these early patterns were adopted almost unchanged in Europe and only modified or formed anew later. We owe it to the grandfather of Meissen painting, Höroldt, that we have great numbers of his personal designs that were based on originals from the Far East. The actual charm of this Indian painting lies in their colorful and ornamental nature. Motif elements and drawings almost never overlap each other. Shadowings are rare, and the contrast of the individual colors to each other stresses their particularly graphic character. We begin with a relatively simple decor using this painting technique (Ill. 97).

a. Stencil the pattern in the described manner. Make sure that all stencil holes are reached by the charcoal and that the entire pattern is thus transferred. As long as all goes well, we now have the motif on the piece in dotted form. If the charcoal has become too dark, blow lightly across the object; that produces a fine, powdery outline which allows drawing with the pen.

b. Now we draw in the contours in the desired color, using the method already described. In the example in Illustration 97b, it is in medium black. Try to achieve an even strength of the stroke and avoid any breaks in the lines, so the motif will not look irregular. If the paint and charcoal should mix with each other during the drawing, this is of no importance, since the charcoal particles will disappear during the firing, leaving no ashes. Try for a light pen stroke that allows no differences in the strength of the lines. Let it dry carefully. An intermediate firing is recommended for beginners.

c. Now we can lay out the resulting surfaces in color and give the decor its own brilliance. Proceed exactly according to the model and be careful to make the color as even as possible. Soft transitions are best achieved with a gentle handling of the color through the use of thin turpentine, which allows an almost perfect blending of the color and white. For larger surfaces, the [Stupfer] is of importance, since it serves ideal in blending the piece and the colored area, especially for garments and natural phenomena such as clouds, fog, water, or even smoke.

In this type of Indian painting, the technique is the simplest one possible. As yet there is no application of a second color or addition of gold attempted. It is very well suited to gaining familiarity with new material.

When one has the possible motifs of Indian painting before his eyes, one soon recognizes what variety is available to us. The Far Eastern masters scarcely omitted any subject, and it can only be an advantage to try out as great a spectrum of the many types as possible. Although the stylization is taken from almost all models, we should nevertheless deal with the various plants and animals, in order to recognize how one in fact simplifies a motif. That means one should come to understand what details one can leave out without making the picture fully unrecognizable.

Every stylized element of a decor has its forerunner in nature. In many parts of a porcelain motif one must look very carefully to recognize the kind of tree or species of animal. Typical characteristics are almost always emphasized, thus giving the painting its own unmistakable character. Evergreen trees often appear lumpy and angular so as to emphasize their sticky nature. The leaves of various broadleaf trees, on the other hand, are kept round and soft. But animals too are shown only in their most important visible characteristics.

Pheasant With Flowers (Ill. 94)

The pheasant in the center of the painting was divided into individual segments in order to separate the different groups of feathers. There are no soft transitions, and the colors were divided into individual fields. The sections on the back are changed into a scaly coat, showing the exact positions of the feathers and their varying colors. The soft coat of down on the breast has become a unified surface, which only takes on some movement thanks to several spots of color. The formation of the splendid tail has also been reduced to the most essential. We recognize the teardrop shapes on the golden yellow feathers. So only the basic representation of a shape or structure is reproduced. The wings, to be sure, are an exception, as are the beak, the eyes, and also the feet. These parts of the body give the motif its necessary naturalness, allowing it to be recognized and understood despite all the abstraction. As for the intensity of color, we can even go a little bit beyond nature, since we want to create colorful, even glaring contrasts. Choose your motifs calmly and familiarize yourself with their shapes and colors. Paint from the hole palette here too, since mixtures may be necessary. This is also advisable when you want to paint several parts.

The flower (Ill. 94) has likewise been strongly simplified and shows relatively identical petal shapes, which differ from each other merely in their tones and rib patterns. The drawing of the blossom and the leaves has been kept in the same shade and thus provides an acceptable framework for the coloring. The excessive use of minor details was avoided, so that drawing, ribbing, soft basic color and a little shadow achieve the effect. Branches and stalks are likewise painted sparingly and show only a few details. After all, the plant is not supposed to distract one from the main motif of the pheasant.

Stylized Flowers (Ill. 97)

Flowers and leaves can be modified into a simplified decor comparatively easily. First of all, the outer contours were drawn in large strokes, round, pointed, oval or long and slim, according to their type. Out of flowers with many circles of petals one forms rosettes with strict symmetry. According to their size, they can have up to seven rings. In 97 you see an example in which three levels are shown.

The complete shape of the stylized flowers has been kept geometric for the most part. We recognize star-shaped, round, or elliptical shapes which merely suggest the basic character of the type.

The first motifs of this type of painting came to Europe from China and Japan. After the foundation of the East India Company in 1624, these pieces passed through Portugal and The Netherlands to many business houses in Europe. There were many underglaze flowers, to which red-gold elements on the glaze were added. The legendary onion pattern, which was taken over after Böttger's invention of European porcelain, also had its origin here. In the decor we recognize stylized flowers such as the chrysanthemum or the forget-me-not. For the manufacturer and collector, various flowers also had a symbolic meaning that made the painted objects more valuable.

98 Indian painting on a gravy boat.

Stylized Animals, Dragons, Imaginary Creatures

In the mythology and legends of the Far Eastern nations, dragons, lions, tigers and imaginary creatures have held important positions for centuries. They are often expressions of anxiety in the face of the unknown or are intended to defeat evil spirits. Often, though, they were simplified portrayals of living animals. To the western observer, these creatures express a definitely exotic and mysterious charm. Who is not familiar with the Ming dragons, that appear to be a mixture of snake, fish, and bird. In a multitude of silk painting, watercolors, woodcuts and porcelain as well, we meet these fantastic creatures which have not lost their charm to this day.

The animal world of the Far East was likewise taken over for the motifs of the porcelain painter and offers us a rich assortment of patterns, such as the rich yellow lion (Ill. 101) designed for the court of Saxony in 1728. In this it is notable that the figure is actually a tiger which has gone through a confusion similar to that of the onion pattern, which portrays pomegranates instead of onions.

Taking the example of the "court dragon" in Illustration 100, I would like to present the creative process of one of the most widespread Indian patterns. From 1730 to 1918, it was painted only for the Saxon court in Dresden, but now

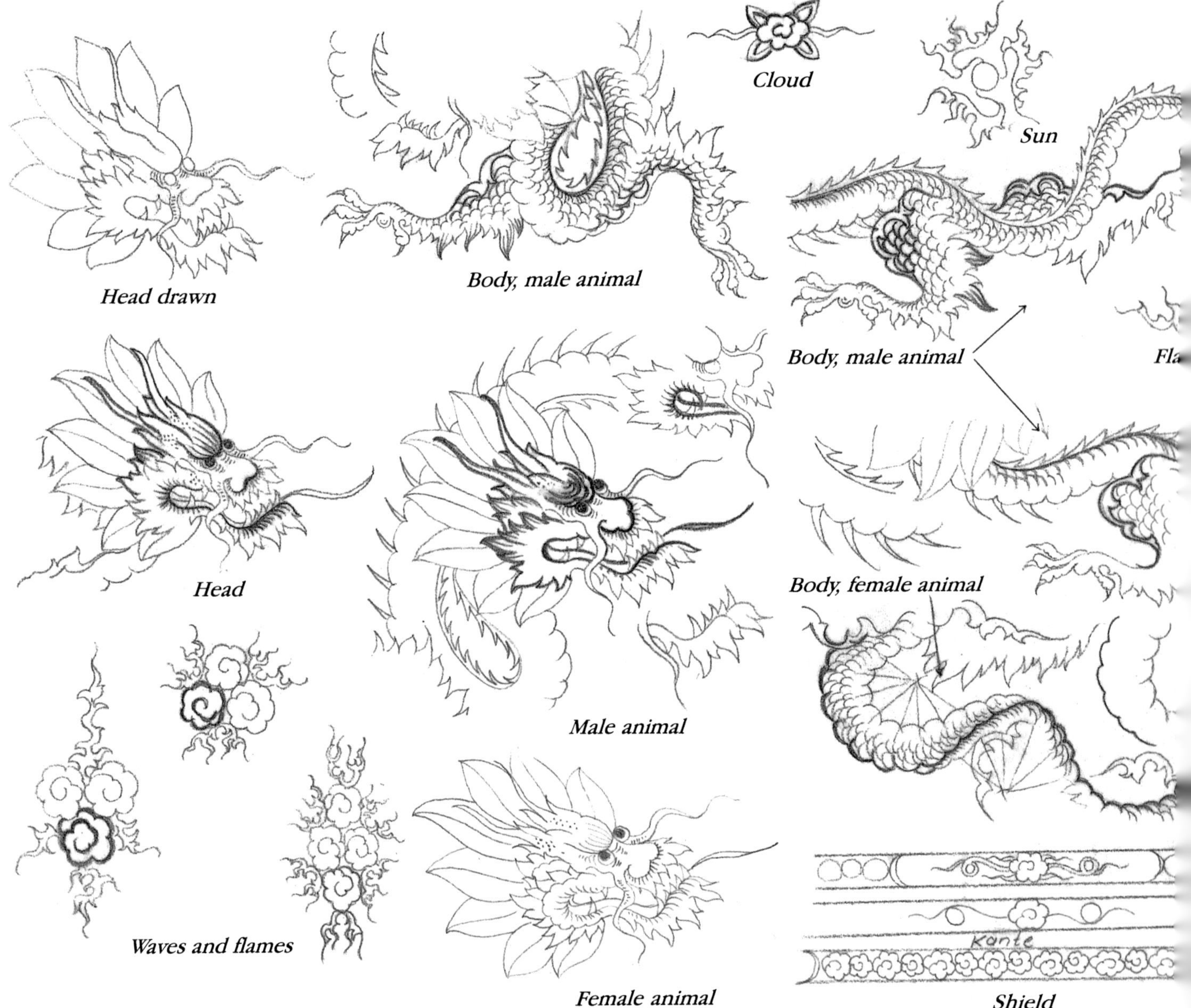

99 Studies for a Ming dragon.

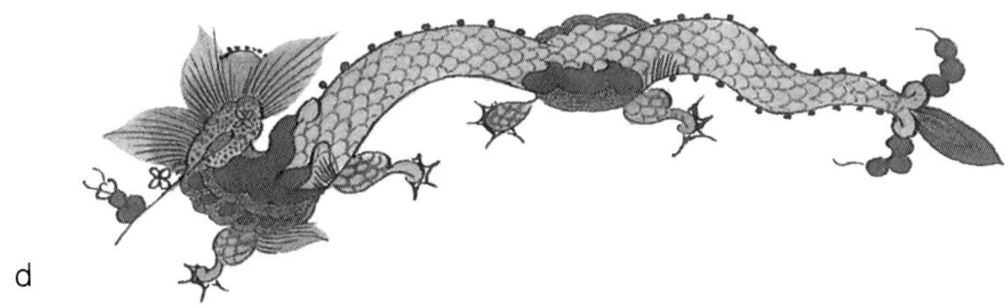

100 The so-called court dragon requires four work processes in all (see text below).

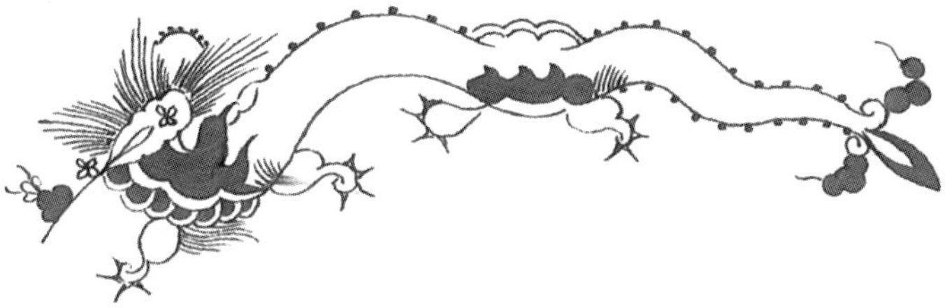

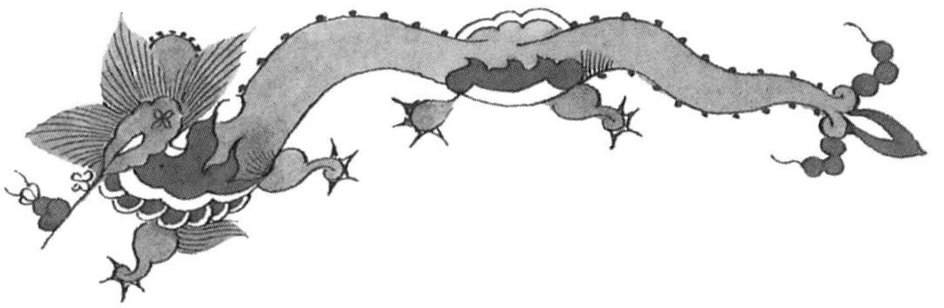

you may feel free to utilize it.

—Lay out the motif on the stencil.

—Stencil the motif onto the cleaned pieces.

a. Draw the outer contours with the pen, in the desired colors.

b. Add the enclosed shadowed surfaces and put in details and elements (with the brush).

c. After letting it dry well, lay out the delineated surfaces in the desired colors. Mix the paint relatively greasy in order to attain a color strength that will remain constant. Work steadily, and try to put the brush down as little as possible.

Now it is time for an intermediate firing (about 800° C), to make sure that the underpainting does not withdraw when the gold scales are added.

d. By "gold scales" we mean the addition of the details like scales or individual hair structures. As a rule, this is done with gold in powdered form. We mix it in the way already described and now apply the desired spots and lines (Ill. 100d). This is done, as before, with the drawing pen, which allows for neat, precise work.

101 A plate with rich Far Eastern painting and stylized tiger.

102 A Ming dragon done in purple.

GOLD DECORATION

Gold has always been a vital material for the decoration and ornamentation of the most varied types of porcelain painting. In the beginning, one added small decorative elements into the decor and made the border of gold. In time, the formation of these borders became more and more pompous and laborious. Porcelain painting was enclosed in decorative borders, almost resembling fine lace, and they afforded it immeasurable charm. Early Chinese-style works show us what great sensitivity was already devoted to this technique in Old China. Naturally, attempts were made in Europe as well to equal the masters of the Far East. In thousands of variations one can see today how broad the spectrum of all the possibilities is. Here we would like to assemble a basic knowledge that will make it possible to vary these decorations from a simple gold rim to a rich gold border. Let us begin with the available types of porcelain gold.

Gloss Gold

This type of porcelain gold is often regarded as overdone and "kitsch" today. This probably has its origins in the meager gold content of the paint and its use in the past. Souvenir cups with often-overdone decorations and their lack of durability for steady use have also done their share. For porcelain objects, that are intended purely for decoration however, this type of gold is thoroughly useful. Gloss gold is also ideal for use as an underlay for polished gold, which will be treated below. Gloss gold has the essential advantage of appearing in the finest nuances after firing without having to undergo additional treatment. In many factories, gloss gold has taken a firm place over the years. The name "gloss gold" was derived from the simple fact that it comes out of the oven with a fine gleaming surface right after firing and does not need to be polished.

Polished Gold

Polished gold is applied in liquid form, just like gloss gold. It is sold in 2-, 5-, 10- and 50-gram bottles. The gold content is considerably higher than that of gloss gold and amounts to about 20%. It is of tough, resinous consistency and is a brownish-black color, so that it can be applied to white porcelain clearly. This is especially important for intricate borders in which thin lines are to be formed. Before being used, polished gold absolutely must be shaken well, since the fine gold particles settle to the bottom of the bottle and thicken somewhat. If it should dry out on the palette during painting, we can easily mix a little turpentine or gold thinner into it. In order to make the polished gold longer-lasting and more valuable, some powdered gold (see the next section) can be added. The polished gold comes out of the firing oven in a matte sand-colored tan, and must now be polished. This is best done with fine sea sand that is taken on a damp cloth and rubbed over the areas to be polished. This works very well under flowing water. It can also be polished with an agate rod, which is set into a wooden handle, or with a glass-fiber brush. Both procedures call for rubbing over the dull gold decor and achieve the desired high gloss. Well-polished gold attains a strong decorative effect and provides a worthy frame for any good painting.

Powdered Gold

As the name itself states, this is a fine gold powder of about 80% purity. Therefore it is naturally remarkably expensive and should be used only for very special borders or tiny details in high-priced decors. It is well suited to use as an additive for polished gold, since it helps the latter attain better durability and longer life. Powdered gold must likewise be polished right after firing. The powder is also mixed, like the metal oxides, with turpentine and thick oil.

Brushes

According to the thickness of gold borders or other gold decorations, we need a certain variety of brushes, plus their handles and sockets. In part, they are made differently from those used for decor painting. The most important types are shown in 103a-c. They are shaped according to their purposes and should be used only for painting in gold. Store these brushes separately too, in a box with cardboard soaked in oil of cloves.

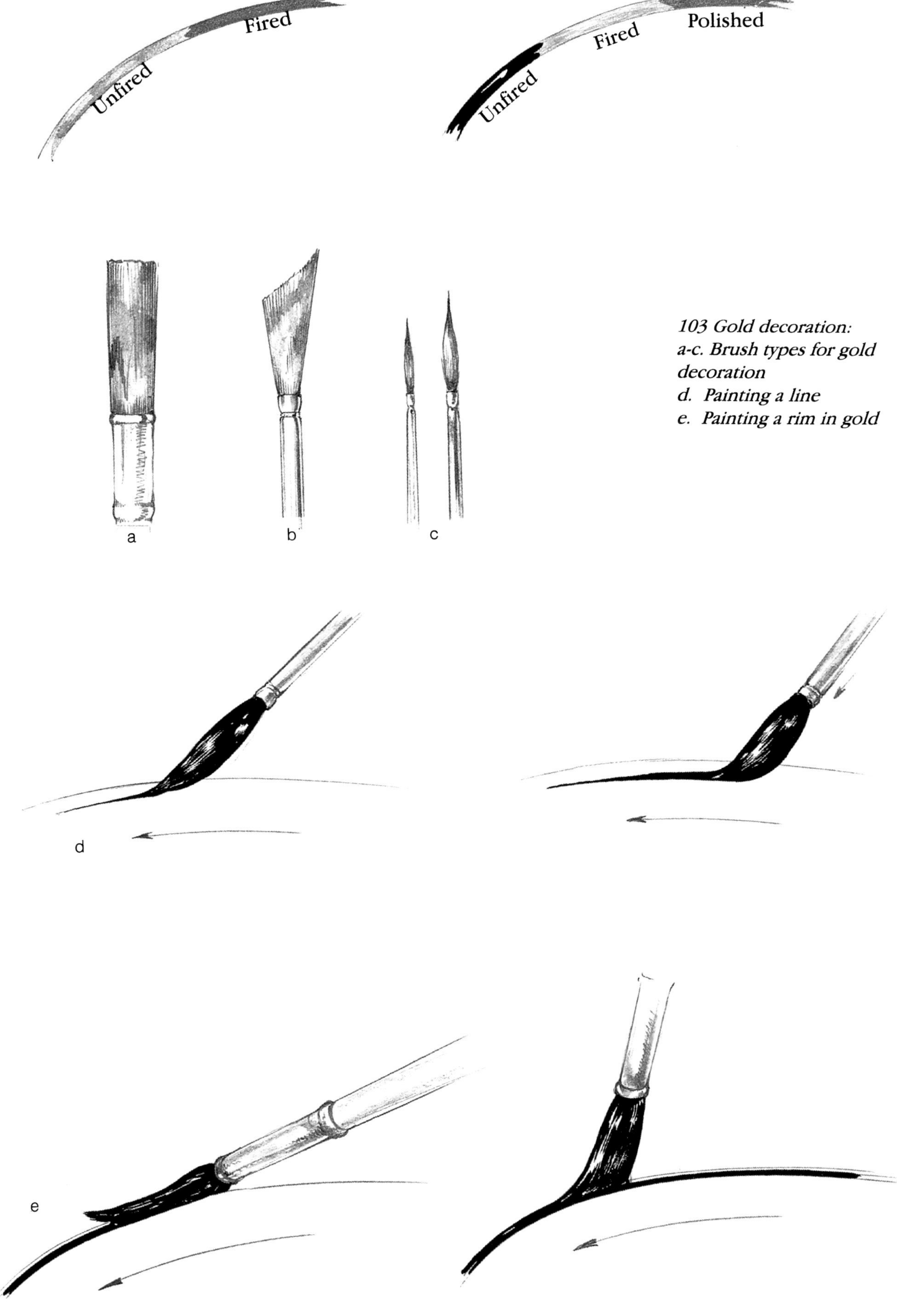

103 Gold decoration:
a-c. Brush types for gold decoration
d. Painting a line
e. Painting a rim in gold

One needs:

a. a flat bristle brush for edging ([Abstreicher]),

b. angle-cut brushes for painting lines, and

c. small decorating brushes for making points on handles, etc.

Border Discs

In order to be able to paint good and, above all, truly round gold bands on plates, platters, bowls, and other flat pieces, we need the border disc. Two types of them can be had. One is the standing type that stands on the floor and can be adjusted as to height, the other is smaller and rests on a table and is especially well suited when a large number of plates are to be rimmed.

Drawing Lines With the Border Disc

The object to be bordered must first be centered on the disc. It must be exactly in the middle to guarantee a faultless border. The hand that holds the brush is supported by the armrest, while the other sensitively turns the disc with the porcelain object on it. When you start, try simple plates without relief patterns, so as to begin by learning to paint a simple golden stripe in circular form. To do this, use brush type b. Carefully take up the polished gold paint with the brush (for practice, ordinary black paint can be used at first). The angled shape of the brush now provides a very good point that is carefully placed at one place on the rotating plate. Begin with a very thin stripe and only make it thicker after about 5 cm (Ill. 103d). After about 7 cm, press the brush down far enough to attain the desired width of the stripe, and then run the stripe all the way around the rim of the plate. If the paint on the brush should run out during this process (which, after some practice, will no longer be the case), just dip the brush in the paint again and set it back on the end of the stripe. Naturally, borders on the rims of very curved or patterned plate rims cause problems, for we have to follow the shape of the rim. This calls for a lot of fingertip feeling and practice, since the plate has to be moved constantly. Here too, practice with paint first, and on plates with simple reliefs.

Painting the Border

For the rims of plates, pots, cups and other porcelain, we need brush type a. This is a wide-bristle brush, which can also be made of soft squirrel hair. Now we are painting borders on the outer rims of dishes. It is important, particularly for larger pieces, to work smoothly, so that the starting and stopping points are not noticeable. The outer or upper rim around the piece is always painted first, and then the finishing lower rim (Ill. 103e). This is especially important for plates. The rims of vases, teapots, tureens, or other large pieces, on the other hand are considerably harder to gild. Often they have oval or curving rims that demand a gentle touch in putting on or taking off the brush. Here we use the floor disc, which allows us to adjust its height.

Framing Medallions and Backgrounds

A rim of gold is also suitable for paintings in the bottoms of plates. If the bottom does not have round edges that can be painted on the disc, then we must paint freehand (Ill. 51-53). Bows, bends, or other ornaments can thus be painted with brush type c. Particular care is required for this type of gold decoration, since, for example, a cobalt blue bottom already looks very dark, and the blackish gold is hard to discern on the blue background. Powdered gold would be ideal for use here, since it already shows an ochre tone when being painted and thus stands out clearly from the dark-colored background. Light background tones, on the other hand, cause no difficulties. A yellow spotted background contrasts very well with the deep black of the polished gold. If you want to apply elaborate gold borders to plate bottoms, then proceed as described in the next section which deals with lavish and filigree lace borders.

Gold Borders

Depending on the motif (hunting scenes, landscapes, still-lifes with fruit, etc.), elaborate gold borders worked out to the smallest detail may be suitable. They are made primarily of polished gold. Their precise nature is not prescribed, although certain types are described as "hunting borders" or "fruit frames" in the literature of porcelain. Let us look somewhat more closely at the basic composition of such a border.

Here we find a certain symmetry that is repeated around a piece of porcelain. Let us begin

104 Several examples of gold borders, which demand a lot of work but liven up a piece considerably.

with a simple rim for a jewelry box (Ill. 105a). At first the oval is divided into four equal segments. Within such a quarter we now determine the exact pattern of the border. Within one quarter we can still make about three divisions (1). In each of these thirds we place the basic motif of the border. In all, it is repeated twelve times around the edge. This preliminary drawing (2) is done with the crayon. Now the painting begins with a brush (3). At first we work out the flourishes and fine details of the band. Only at the end do we enclose everything with a gold stripe at the rim (4).

In all gold painting it is important to keep it extremely clean, as even insufficiently removed unsuccessful attempts can cause disturbing flecks. Light pink smears are the result.

You can also use your own cloths and thinner containers for work in gold. How far you want to go with various other borders is up to you. You will find ideas in Illustration 104.

Decorating Handles, Spouts, and Knobs

The placing of ornamentation is made relatively simple for us in most of the elements of porcelain pieces. Many edges, reliefs, or designs really invite one to paint them. We touch them up lightly with the brush and thus give them an unimposing decoration (Ill. 105b-d). It is also possible to draw with the pen or apply an ostentatiously overloaded baroque decor. But we should not forget that all gold decoration has only an underlining character and should really em-

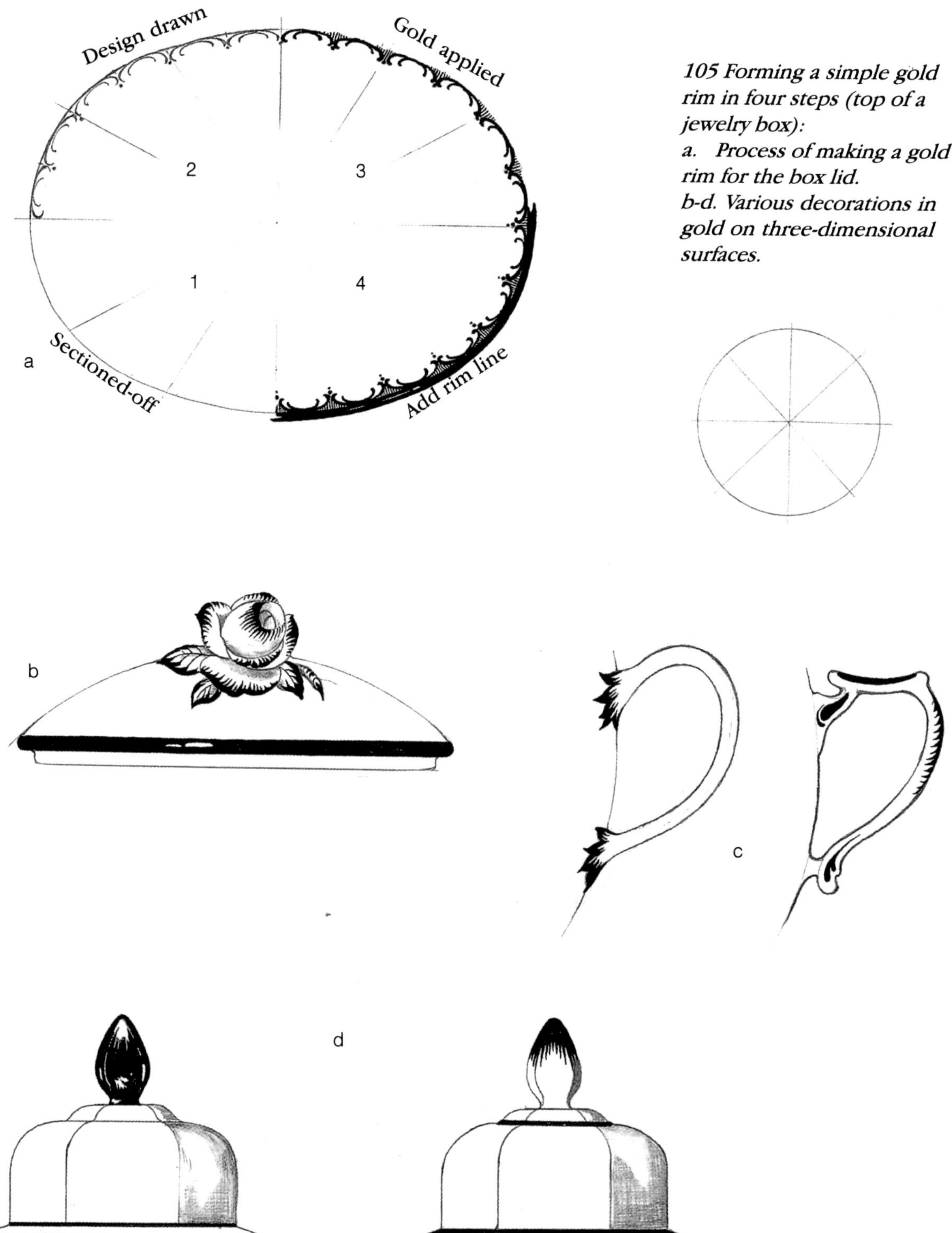

105 Forming a simple gold rim in four steps (top of a jewelry box):
a. Process of making a gold rim for the box lid.
b-d. Various decorations in gold on three-dimensional surfaces.

phasize or beautify the primary decoration. Too much gold easily achieves a purely metallic impression and turns one away from a piece that could have made a good impression.

When painting large surfaces, one should work smoothly and steadily, so as to achieve a smooth, completely regular paint job. The greatest amount of gold ornamentation is undoubtedly that of figures, which should not concern us here. To be sure, we can learn from a great many porcelain figures how small projections, decorations, minute details, and pedestals are gilded. I would also like to take this opportunity to mention literature and museums in which we can obtain a wealth of inspiration. Collecting brochures and catalogs from fairs and exhibitions is also recommended. Nor should one's own wealth of ideas and joy in experimenting be forgotten. I recommend a slim, not overly short hair brush as the ideal type.

Things like knobs on covered vases are often decorated with simple borders and rings too. The border disc also helps us here.

The decoration of longish elements, such as coffeepot handles, is considerably more difficult. Often one must make a rather long stroke that must also be even in width and color. Another factor is the sometimes bad handling of larger pieces, such as tureens, pitchers or even candlesticks. One must be especially careful so as not to damage whatever colored decor may already be present. Working with fine cloth gloves has proved to be very useful here, since one can thus avoid contact between paint and damp hands. If the piece has already been protected by an early firing, then one can go ahead and gild it safely.

What type of gold ornamentation is used depends, of course, on the piece to be decorated. The many prescribed styles do not allow a colorful, kitschy mess. Find out what era the piece belongs to or is based on. One cannot decorate a strict Art Nouveau design with opulent Baroque art.

All of these decorative possibilities can also be done in colors. In many old examples one can see how charming a purple or even a brownish border can look. Many paintings are enhanced more by such colored decoration than by gold. For example, think of hunting scenes or even Chinese designs. But here too, one's personal taste should set the standards. Three-dimensional knobs like roses, fruits, flourishes, or animals can likewise be painted in color and create a successful link to the decor itself. Surely the devoted porcelain admirers among you have already seen the type of knob that portrays a cut lemon. Decorating this in gold would be really foolish, as the relatively large fruit would appear too heavy and imposing and thus weaken the entire piece. Small roses and handles in all imaginable forms, on the other hand, can stand modest and finely applied decoration in gold very well (Ill. 105b, c).

Gilding Pierced Porcelain

Porcelain pieces with partially pierced rims, such as platters, vases, or various figures, demand great patience and delicate feeling from the painter. Often the finest, almost lacelike piercings have to be decorated. This additional ornamentation of dish parts has existed for a long time, and the production of such pieces caused great difficulties for many years, since such thin rims often drooped under hot firing at over 1000° C and made the rim of the plate look crooked and unsightly. Porcelain manufacturers only seldom have such problems today, and you have a variety of pieces to choose from.

The gilding itself is made easy on many pieces, since it is generally a plaited design whose raised sections we can recognize very easily and need only decorate with gold.

But there are also imaginative, fantastic pierced edges that demand precise contouring. Flowers and very small decorative elements in three-dimensional form also turn up often. These must not necessarily be decorated in gold, but can just as well be done in colors.

There are also plates that have three to five spaces in their pierced rims, to which one can apply small paintings. These can also be done in gold or in colors.

Gold decorations can be done with the brush or the pen. Polished gold is ideally suited here, and powdered gold is best for very small lines drawn with a pen. For the polishing that follows, the agate rod is excellent, since we must reach many arches and curves, and these places are not easy to reach with a glass brush.

PLATINUM DECORATION

Gloss or polished platinum, like gloss or polished gold, can be obtained in liquid form and is the equal of gold in use and characteristics. The main difference is the somewhat different realm in which it is used. The highly polished silver or even chrome effect is more likely to be found in the modern varieties of porcelain art, although this precious-metal color has been in existence for some time. Platinum is especially suitable for Art Nouveau motifs or abstract paintings, nor should we forget the broad realm of its use in heraldry. Many services with coats of arms and symbols of nobility require a certain amount of silver-colored elements. Just as with the two types of gold, we much polish the polished platinum after firing, while the gloss platinum comes out of the oven looking almost like a mirror.

Use the same tools and brush as for gold decoration, and store the platinum implements separately. Turpentine, thinner, and thick oil are used as before in preparing the paint.

Platinum is very expensive, and therefore it should be used only sparingly and cautiously. It also has a particularly elegant effect when, for example, it is used only for borders of plates or decoration of certain figures. I urge you not to overdo its use, since here too it can quickly produce an unwanted metallic atmosphere. Objects decorated completely with platinum all too easily look like cheap plastic imitations. Painting porcelain objects with both gold and platinum should also be avoided. The impression of an overdecorated "sea of precious metal" can be created all too easily.

Platinum harmonizes very well with black, as well as with pure white. Outstanding effects can also be achieved with platinum on porcelain glazed in black. There is a whole series of figures that have been ornamented only sparingly and thus achieve an ideal combination of black and chromelike elegance.

The use of platinum is also particularly suitable for the formation of monograms. Combined with a decorative wreath around the plate, the name in script, or just the initials, of the host produce a worthy frame for a formal, festive dinner party. In what way you use platinum is again left up to you, and you can use all you want of the available spectrum. The precise application is the same as that of gold decoration.

MONOGRAMS

The decoration of individual plates or entire services with monograms has enjoyed great popularity for many years. Often the initials of a restaurant, or of the host of a private festivity, were used as a sign of the finest dining. Occasionally one also encounters combinations of signatures and finely painted coats of arms. The type of script to be chosen should naturally match the style of the porcelain. There are striking Art Nouveau styles of script, just as there are classic, Baroque, modern, and abstract scripts, any of which can be used as needed to go with the object. The choice is tremendous, and now the decision is up to your own taste.

The surroundings in which the piece is to be seen often plays a decisive role. Rustic restaurants will certainly use a very different type of monogram from modern bars and cafes. The precise arrangement of the letters or coat of arms depends on the use of the dish. The edge of a plate is a popular place, as is the middle of the plate. Variations which have various letters in a border or a corner are also possible. Select the most suitable variation for you by experimenting on the porcelain with the crayon.

The choice of colors can include practically all variations, although gold and platinum letters enjoy great popularity. If a colored border enhances the plate, though, then the monogram can also be applied in a suitable shade.

The technique of application is relatively simple. You draw the chosen script or the individual letters thinly at first. If freehand drawing causes you trouble, then a stencil can be used here. Take the application of the paint from the previous chapters. Here are a few styles of scripts that have proved to be especially popular and suitable:

—Park Avenue, Aristocrat, Juliet, and Palace Srvipt for modern dishes,

—Apollo, Le Golf, Ringlet, and Davida for Art Nouveau porcelain,

—Koch Fraktur, Old English, Alte Schwabacher, and Walbaum Fraktur for rustic dishes.

Naturally it is also possible to place a whole line of writing, a dedication, or a particular date on a painted porcelain article. It is very popular—especially for use on gifts—to add a brief greeting or a few words in remembrance of a special occasion. Just how you place these words

is up to you. There is a possibility of combining the writing directly with the decor, though it appears kitschy after a time. It is better to place them on the back or underside of the object. Exceptions to this are wall plates or cups that are supposed to carry the text. You are surely familiar with the well-known beer steins that have been produced for various organizations or celebrations. To make them, we can use one of two techniques:

—Pen Drawing

As already described in the *Indian Painting* chapter, the pen is ideally suited to making very thin lines. If it is to be a decorative script with evenly fine lines, this technique is recommended. With appropriate practice, you can form whole sentences smoothly and quickly.

—Brush Writing

This way of painting becomes necessary when the script calls for differing line thicknesses for different letters. Some sorts of letters simply require longer and more intensive use of ornamental and decorative elements. A fine brush is ideally suited to create all the appropriate delicacies.

106 Examples of different types of letters and their arrangement.

107 A simple monogram, in which the letters are slightly offset from each other.

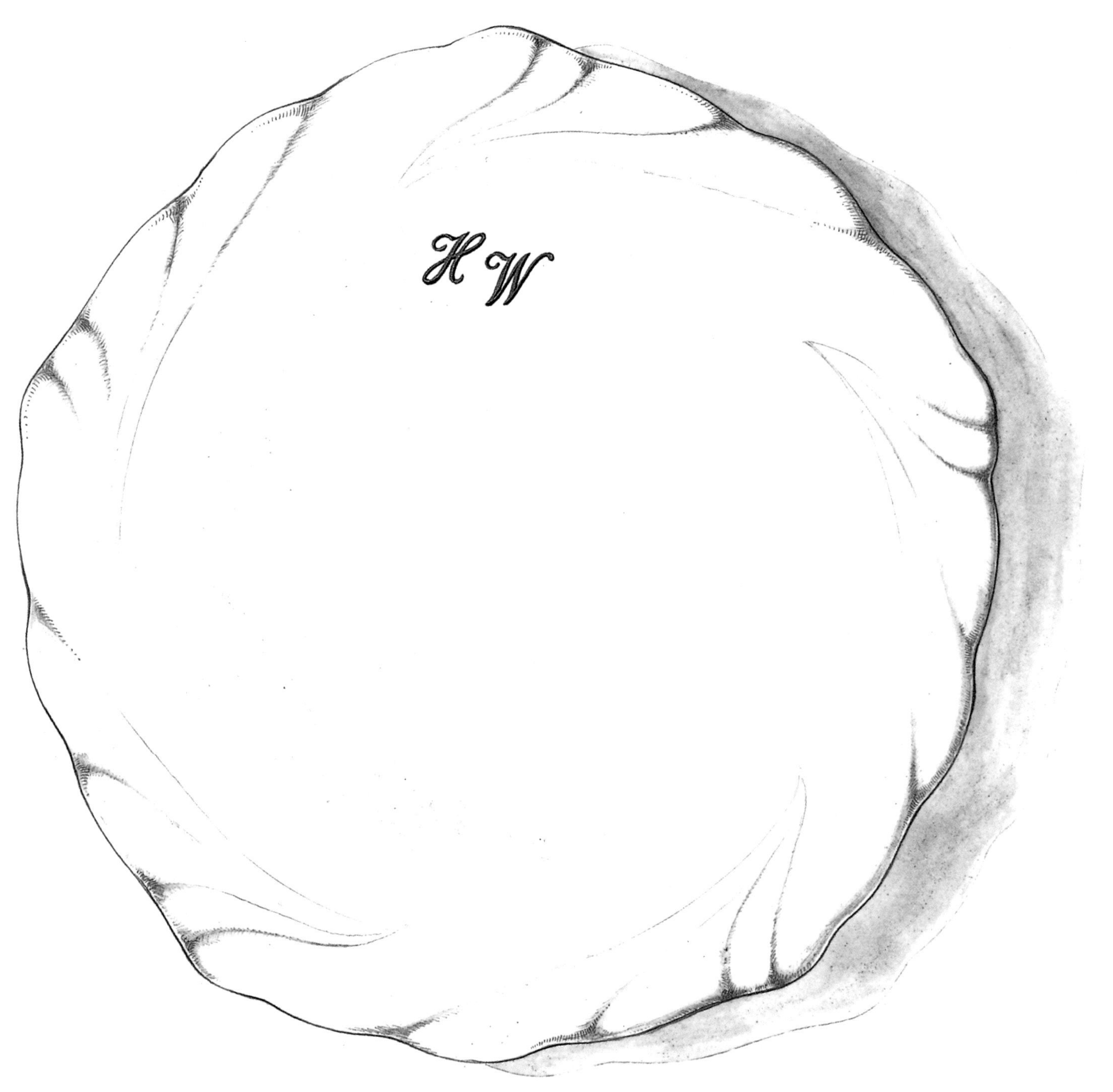

108 Monograms can be located on the rim or in the center, with good effect.

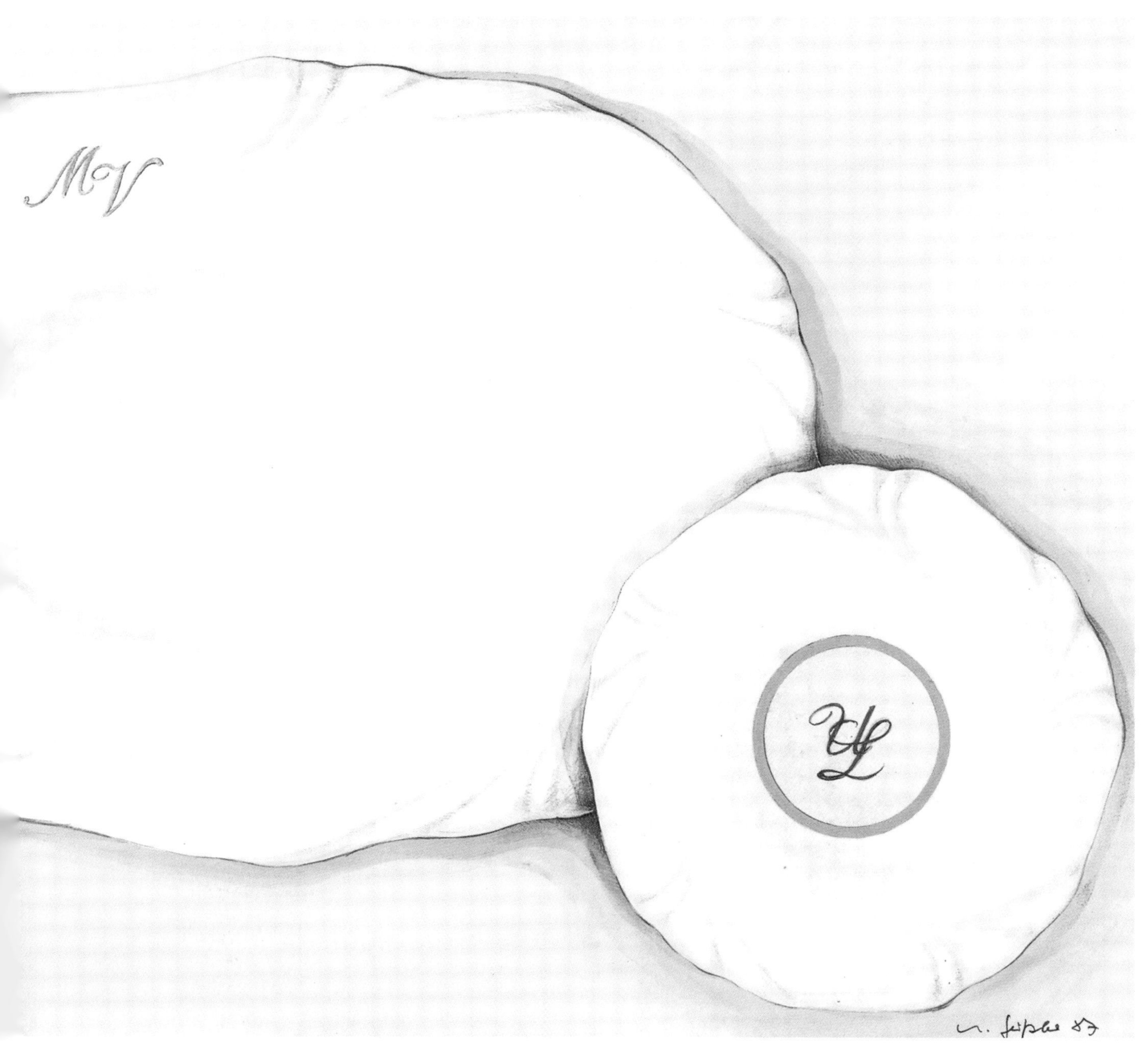

Hotel
mira
Hotel
mira

◁ *109 A hotel signet on a coffee set. The script and colors should be chosen to match those used by the hotel.*

SIGNETS

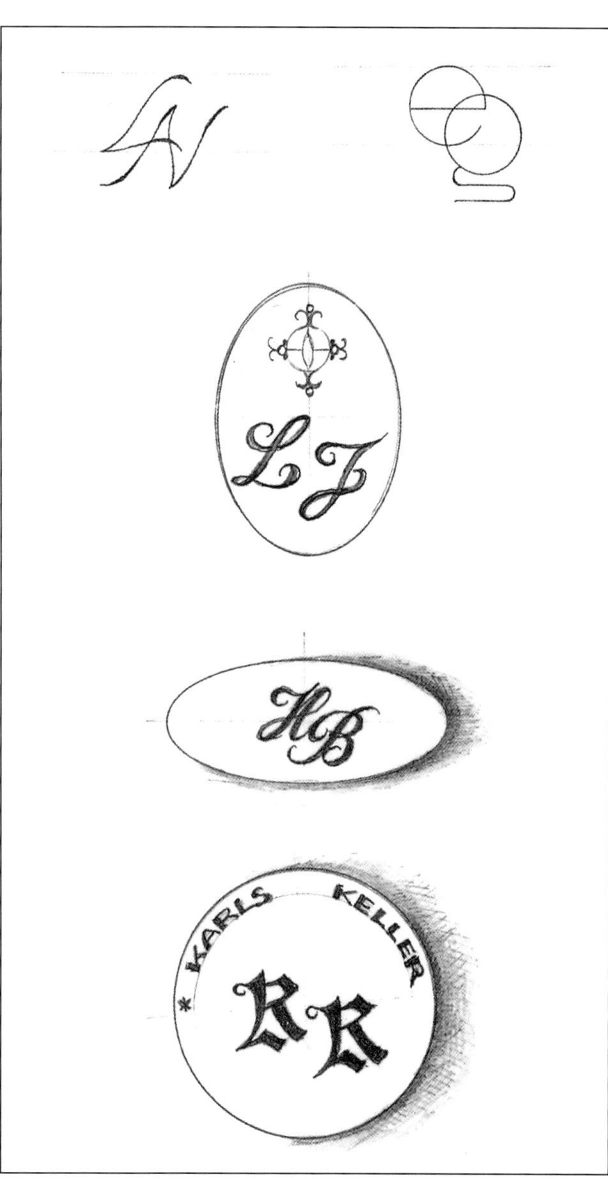

110 Various signets.

Many hotels and restaurants like to decorate their porcelain with an unmistakable emblem or monogram of the hotel name or that of its owner. Since such orders from customers are very rare, I'd like to show you only in brief how this genre is handled. The choice of motifs is taken from you in such cases, since the letters, emblems or certain ornaments are generally determined by the tradition or style of the hotel or restaurant. You simply need to take this signet and transfer it suitably to the pieces of porcelain. The transfer (above all else, in the right scale), is naturally not as simple as it sounds. If you are experienced enough to do the job freehand, you have done well and saved some time too.

It may be somewhat more difficult for the layman, and reducing or enlarging through the use of a photocopier is recommended. Copy the signet from the model (menu or whatever) in the desired size and place it on the object in question. Here there are many chances to use frames, ornaments, gold effects, etc.

Base what you do on the original or on the wishes of the current proprietor. In the example in Illustration 109, the hotel name is framed in an ochre-colored oval which in turn is held in a red-brown band. The use of gold, or the signet as a whole, was ordered by the customer. It can often be seen that hotels include gold decorative elements. If these should be gold segments on a colored background, I recommend that you paint the colored background first and then do an intermediate firing, in order to make the later addition of the gold easier.

EXAMPLES OF PORCELAIN PAINTING

111 One of many possible variations of a motif expressing good wishes. The script itself can naturally be done in gold or platinum as well.

112 Simple flower painting with gold grass.

114 A rose painted with forget-me-nots on a swan's-neck cup. ▷

113 Fruit painting in a style based on the old techniques of the still-life painters of The Netherlands.

115 Whether a tea bowl or a candlestick, with skillful decoration the details are ever so beautiful. ▷

116 An example of light, airy flower painting in just three colors (poppy pattern).

117 Poppy decor; note that the cup decor continues into the interior of the cup.

118 A coffee cup with floral surface decor, with which flawed white porcelain can also be painted, as flawed spots are easy to conceal.

119 A tasteful sight on the coffee table: fruits and flowers.

120 Naturalistic fruit painting (forest fruits) is particularly suitable for coffee and tea services.

121 Indian painting at its noblest: this "Silver Bird" motif was painted in platinum.

GLOSSARY

Agate Rod
A semiprecious stone of the finest structure, with which one can polish matte gold to an elegant high gloss.

Armrest
A raised surface area for the painter's arm that holds the brush. The U-shaped cutout in it allows optimal holding of the object to be painted.

Background
An even single-color surface, which can also include white cutouts.

Bone China
English bone porcelain, in which the calcium phosphate derived from burned cattle bones acts as a flux.

Bubbling
Reaction of the paint when applied too thickly. Bubbles or cracks result after firing.

Chinese Style
Pictures based on Chinese life and culture, often detracted from by added European details.

Composition
A tasteful arrangement of a decor on the porcelain object. The shape, style and color harmony should be considered.

Covering Paint
A thick liquid mass that, after being applied, hardens to a stiff sheet and can be removed without trouble.

Decor
Decorating a white piece of porcelain in one or more colors. Hand -painted or stamped decors of all kinds can be used. Colored and gilded borders, and various glazing techniques, can also be included.

Decoration
Decoration of three-dimensional elements of dishes and figures.

Flux
A substance that lowers the melting point of a paint, glaze, or other substance (red lead, lead carbonate).

Laying On
The second step, after outlining, in which the essential elements of the motif are applied in color.

Medium
Substances used to prepare the powdered pigment, such as turpentine, oil of cloves, thickened balsam, and so-called "Zach oil" (turpentine in solidified resin).

Assay furnace
An electrically operated melting oven with thick insulating walls. At the top there is usually a steam outlet, and there is a peephole in the door. The heating coils generally run along the inner walls.

Oil Thickener
Up to three dishes, one inside another, in which turpentine slowly thickens into thick oil.

Oxide Pigments
Porcelain pigments that are made out of metal oxides and melt well when burned when the appropriate flux is added.

Pâte-sur-Pâte Painting
A complex technique of porcelain decoration. The motifs are made in almost relief form and often painted in soft pastel tones.

Pieces
Collective term for porcelain objects of all kinds.

Rim
The outer rim of the plate, from the outside in to the fallaway to the inner area (Tellerspiegel).

Squirrel Hair
The finest brush hair, from the tail of a Siberian squirrel.

Stencil
An aid to quicker drawing of the motif pattern. It is usually made of metal foil into which the contours of the pattern are pin-pricked. Through these holes, charcoal is put on the piece. Especially suitable for beginners and for painting large quantities with the same pattern (*Indian Painting*).

Strewing
Small decor elements (flowers, insects, fruits, etc.) to decorate the object around the main motif, or used for the unobtrusive disguising of small flaws in the piece or the glaze.

Stylizing
Simplification or transposition of naturalistic motifs.

Surface Decor
A painting or stamping that includes the entire white surface of a porcelain piece and thus scarcely leaves any white surfaces (especially suitable for flawed pieces).

Working Out
Completing the layout with all required details such as shadows, glazing and inscriptions.

BIBLIOGRAPHY

Friedel, Peter, Porzellan und Keramik Bemalen—mein Hobby, Munich 1982.

Hillebrecht, Bente, & Schmidt, Janet, Porzellanmalerei, Stuttgart 1987.

Imhof, Phyllis, Aparte Porzellanmalerei, Freiburg 1985.

Jaennicke, Friedrich, Handbuch der Porzellan-, Steingut- und Fayance-Malerei, Stuttgart 1987 (reprint of 1891 edition).

Kesten, Brigitte, Charakteristik der Porzellanfarben, Stuttgart 1984.

Kretschmar-Volck, Hedwig, Porzellanmalerei, Stuttgart 1984.

Lumm, Rudolf, Porzellanmalerei, Stuttgart 1984.

Mields, Martin, Praxis der Porzellanmalerei, Munich 1965.

Viggiani, Daniella, Die kunst der Porzellanmalerei, Stuttgart 1985.

PHOTO CREDITS

All the drawings shown in this book were prepared by the author except 2, 69, 70, 85 and 111-121, which were prepared by Günther von Voithenberg.